ACCIDENTAL THEOLOGIANS

Accidental Theologians
Four Women Who Shaped Christianity

ELIZABETH A. DREYER

Franciscan
MEDIA
Cincinnati, Ohio

Cover design by Kathleen Lynch | Black Kat Design
Book design by Mark Sullivan

LIBRARY OF CONGRESS CATALOGING-IN-PUBLICATION DATA
Dreyer, Elizabeth, 1945-
Accidental theologians : four women who shaped Christianity / Elizabeth A. Dreyer.
pages cm
Includes bibliographical references.
ISBN 978-1-61636-514-1 (alk. paper)
1. Christian women saints. 2. Women in the Catholic Church. 3. Hildegard, Saint, 1098-1179. 4. Catherine, of Siena, Saint, 1347-1380. 5. Teresa, of Avila, Saint, 1515-1582. 6. Thérèse, de Lisieux, Saint, 1873-1897. I. Title.
BX4656.D74 2014
282.092'52—dc23
2014016013
ISBN 978-1-61636-514-1

Published by Franciscan Media
28 W. Liberty St.
Cincinnati, OH 45202
www.FranciscanMedia.org

Printed in the United States of America.
Printed on acid-free paper.
14 15 16 17 18   5 4 3 2 1

CONTENTS

by Joan Chittister

We create for ourselves two equally limiting visions of life when we divide up the world into categories of "past" and "present." First, we tend to valorize one and ignore the other. And second, the division is not true and cannot really be done. Those are the reasons this book needed to be written, and those are the reasons that it is important to read it.

When we succumb to the temptation to divide the past from the present, the far too common long-term effect is that concentrating on the past tends to shrivel the mind, to chain its insights, to narrow its vision.

On the other hand, when we act as if the world were created yesterday and is ours to define out of whole cloth, irrespective of where today came from, there is an equal danger. Knowing nothing about where our present ideas or ideologies came from, caring little about either the insights that underlie them or the ramifications they suggest, we will lack any vision for where we need to go now.

Neither position is tenable. Or as the wag wrote somewhere, the difference between conservatives and liberals is that "conservatives prefer foolishness hallowed by time while liberals prefer their foolishness fresh off the vine." There is enough foolishness in both to go around. There is also enough wisdom in each to demand our awareness, to save us from the excesses of both.

The wisdom of the world cannot simply be defined as only past or present because one leads to the other—the past has created the present. More than that, we need an understanding of the past in order to find our way through the limitations of the past to the best of the age that is dawning.

The fundamental truth is that the past has a great deal to teach us, if we will only interrogate it with the future in mind. And the present has a great responsibility to stretch the wisdom of the past in such a way that the best of it is kept and its time-boundedness culled. Otherwise the perspectives of the old, formed out of another time and place, might well smother the emerging gifts of the present.

In these tensions lie the strengths of Elizabeth Dreyer's present book, *Accidental Theologians: Four Women Who Shaped Christianity.*

Dreyer does three things that make this book a treasure: First, she examines both the character of the times and the quality of theology of the four women doctors of the church. This plaiting of time and place gives the theology they teach both substance and reference. This is not theology woven out of the abstract. This theology arises from the temper of the times. This is a lived theology made real by the very environment in which it emerges and to which it responds.

Second, she gives back to the church one of the great gifts of women. She presents women theologians—doctors of the church, no less—who descend from the realms of academic language to help us sense and experience and realize the searing presence of God in daily life. In the language of the time itself, they reveal God-with-us then as now, now as then, in our own dialects, in our own lives. In them, theology is not a foreign language. It is the God-life as they experienced it in the vernacular of their own particular eras.

Finally, it confirms that the body of theology each of these women leaves us is a genuine part of the tradition, true to God's presence in their time yet still alive to God's presence now. It makes us living participants in the history of Christian consciousness. More than that, it frees us to do the same in our own age.

By using every chapter to have us examine our own lived experience of God and our own tongue for explaining common Christian concepts, we become one with the history of the Church. By tracing the eternal stream of Christian understanding and responses under the language and circumstances of each period, we find ourselves fully aware of the presence of the God of life in each.

This plaiting of time and circumstances and understandings of God in past times with the same God impulses in our own gives us the tools to deepen our present consciousness of God in tune with the consciousness of the ages before us. Like the binding of the proverbial shafts of grain, this connection to the past makes us stronger as we go, surer as we grow, and more truly faithful to the past as well as to the present, to the present as well as to the past.

This book draws an arc between past and present that can make a reader more committed to both without abandoning either. It is a gift of thoughts worth reading more than once if, for no other reason than the opportunity to understand the theological connection between what went before us and the awareness of what is coming.

Most of all, it makes "accidental theologians" of us all. Its gift lies in its clear message that we are all meant to be theologians of the heart, the kind of God-seekers who know who it is they seek and why and how. For in that case, we cannot be seduced to idolize any period of theology but find in all of them both a foreshadowing of our own as well as another kind of eternal light to guide us through its darkness.

I thank Franciscan Media, and the many staff members who worked on this book. Special thanks go to Lisa Biedenbach, for generating the idea and inviting me to write this book on the theologies of the four women Doctors of the Church. It has been a privilege and a joy to spend my career delving into the spiritual and theological writings of Christian women across the centuries. I continue to be instructed, moved, and edified by their lives and work. Thus, it is a welcome and deep pleasure to share and interpret these texts for other seekers who desire to broaden their knowledge of the Tradition to include women, discover female role models in the faith, and enhance their own theologies in light of this material.

The importance of laity (especially women) doing theology cannot be stressed enough. While few of us are professional theologians, we are all called by baptism to study and reflect on our lives in the light of the Good News. Twenty-five years ago, I wrote: "To the extent that each of us refuses to reflect on, and speak about, our faith experience, to that extent is theology stunted and incomplete."[1] As the force of Vatican II's inclusion of the laity has receded, the need for grassroots theologians is even more pressing.

The high level of education in our culture makes it possible for many to explore who God is; who we are as God's creatures; how we choose to respond to divine love; and what it means to lead an ethical life. Each in her or his own way responds to the call to be grassroots theologians, empowered by the Holy Spirit to engage in the Christian theological conversation that has been going on since the first century. Since the women you are about to encounter did not have access to formal theological education, they are excellent models for doing theology beyond the academy. Their intelligence and courage help us see the importance of theological reflection and instruct and inspire us to "do theology" more faithfully.

The intellectual astuteness of their thought, however, makes their work a worthy object of study by the entire community—something we have just begun to realize. Elizabeth Johnson notes how a hardening of the mind against unwanted wisdom (such as theology done by women) wrongly limits what we think of as theology. God-talk in relation to women's flourishing should not be pushed to the periphery of serious consideration in the academy, Church, or society. Such refusal of insight due to group bias has only one remedy: conversion of mind and heart.[2]

These women Doctors of the Church had a keen eye for what they perceived as the spiritual emptiness of much scholastic theology. For example, Catherine criticized theologians who chased "after a multiplicity of books, never tasting the marrow of Scripture because they have let go of the light by which Scripture was formed and proclaimed."[3] But we would be wrong to conclude that the use of rigorous logic and reason is not required for doing theology. While one theologian emphasizes logic and another the affections (both of which are subject to error and excess), no authentic theology can be devoid of head or heart. Being moved by God's loving beauty and being clear and orderly in our expression of this love belong together.

I emphasize the importance of context for each author. Because we cannot fully understand and interpret texts from a distant historical past without learning about the contours of that past, I have included sections on the social, cultural, geographic, political, ecclesial, and economic setting of each author. To lift a medieval text, for example, out of its "housing" in twelfth-century Germany is to risk missing the rationale, intent, and meaning of a text altogether.

A second interest is practical and methodological. Presuming that the point of historical study is to enhance our present lives and communities, we need to read, understand, and use them in a responsible, open, and critical way. Things that may have made perfect sense in nineteenth-century Lombardy may not only be unhelpful, but may even be dangerous in twenty-first-century America. The depth and beauty of this material demands that we open ourselves to being transformed by it, but also that we ask hard questions about things that are foreign or even repulsive to us.

A third focus of this study is gender. Given that the history of Christian theology has been built on the exclusion of women, their presence in the theological canon calls for critical reflection on the shape of theology written by women; how their work provides a broader concept of what theology is; and who qualifies as a theologian. We know that Christian women have been stereotyped and marginalized for millennia, and those who chose to write endured an even higher level of skepticism and silencing. Their survival was often due to support from, and collaboration with, male colleagues who had the power and the commitment to make sure their voices were heard. But this does not diminish the courage and perseverance required to follow God's call in difficult circumstances.

That so many texts written by Christian women have survived is an incalculable blessing. That we are charged with the privileged task of gleaning their theological ideas from this material is a joy. It does not erase the immense sadness at the tragic loss of their words, images, music, spiritualities, and theologies, obliterated or never even created because the world judged women unable or unfit to contribute to the higher reaches of cultural and ecclesial life. Their voices, because they are so rare, take on an importance incommensurate with the volume of their production. But they make up for this minority status with their intense zeal, creative insight, and dogged commitment to teach others the "word" that God spoke to them. It is clear that they have a meaningful, life-giving word for our time and we will be mining their theological thought for decades to come. As one woman said at a recent workshop on medieval women mystics: "They are back!"

I thank Deborah Spaide and John Bennett for reading and commenting on the entire text. Their insights and suggestions have made this a much better book. Rose Marie Conway (d. 2013) and Steven Payne read and offered feedback on individual chapters.

CHAPTER ONE

Women Doctors of the Church: Fresh Theological Voices

The naming of Hildegard of Bingen in 2012 as the fourth female Doctor of the Church is the catalyst for this exploration of the theologies of these four women theologians and wisdom figures. This recognition of women as Doctors of the Church is a new chapter in the Church's history, inaugurated by Pope Paul VI, who added the names of Teresa of Avila and Catherine of Siena to the list of Doctors in 1970.

As we will see, none of these women was a theologian in the formal sense of the term; as indicated by the title of the book, they are "accidental theologians." But all were truly exceptional teachers who reflected on and absorbed the Scriptures; lived the Christian life in creative and full ways; and wrote about major theological topics with passion and insight. The theological classics of any tradition are not static relics frozen in time, but are living, breathing documents intended to be read and pondered anew in each generation.

What Is a Doctor of the Church?

The title "Doctor of the Church" has been bestowed by the Roman Catholic Church on thirty-five saintly individuals acknowledged for their outstanding interpretation and teaching of Scripture and Christian doctrine.[1] The term "Doctor of the Church" first came into use between 400 and 600 C.E. It was associated with illustrious figures, mostly bishops, from the early Church, such as Athanasius, Basil, Ambrose, and Augustine. These "fathers of the Church" developed and protected doctrine, sorting out what would become "orthodox" and what "heretical" positions.

The list of Doctors remained fluid into the medieval period when figures such as Anselm of Canterbury, Bernard of Clairvaux, Bonaventure of Bagnoregio, and Thomas Aquinas were added. Aquinas noted that the primary Doctor of the Church was always Christ, while our ability to receive Christ's teaching depended on the Holy Spirit who inspired both ordinary Christians and a small group of distinguished teachers. By the thirteenth century, the papacy assumed more control over the naming of saints and doctors whose lives were officially celebrated in the liturgy along with the apostles and evangelists.

Later, Benedict XIV (d. 1758) established three criteria: (1) service to the Church in the form of profound theological knowledge, including insight into the Scriptures; (2) holiness of life; (3) official Church approval by pope or council. In other words, Doctors of the Church are recognized not only for living the Gospel, but for giving it expression, and for integrating theological wisdom and the spiritual life. When women were added to this group, a fourth criterion was added: The witness and testimony of the saints were seen as a source for theology. This idea was grounded in Vatican II's declaration that the Spirit was at work in the entire People of God. Doctrine could no longer be seen solely in terms of intellect, but must also reflect the existential, daily engagement in the spiritual life which influenced the life of the Church and its theology.

Along with other Christian denominations, Roman Catholicism has worked to unite head and heart, knowledge and faith, reason and love. The mystery of Christ is best entered into and plumbed for meaning in ways that engage the whole person. In this sense, we can think of full theological knowledge as wisdom. Wisdom weds the work of reason, study, and intellect with a life of passionate commitment to Christ and virtuous love. In the case of the four women Doctors of the Church, who had no access to formal advanced education, we have theologies that reveal their significant native intellectual gifts, but which are notably grounded in graced experiential knowledge linked to their intense engagement with God.

For most of Christian history, no one would have thought of separating theology from holiness. But as intellectual tools became more sophisticated and theology was divided into various specialties in the fourteenth century, formal academic knowledge and mystical knowledge were nudged apart. With the development of science and math in the seventeenth century and the age of reason in the eighteenth, reason was seen as the superior and for some, the only path to knowledge. Experiential, affective, emotional and sensual knowledge were relegated to an inferior position.

Of the thirty-five Doctors of the Church, 12 percent are women.[2] Papal recognition of this title was first given by Boniface VIII in 1298.[3] As our experience, understanding, and language for God grows and develops in response to the pressing needs of the day, so too has the concept of "Doctor of the Church" evolved. Since feminism has nurtured a new awareness of women and their role in society and Church, it is not surprising that our understanding of the term *Doctor* would expand to include illustrious women in the Christian tradition. There has been a great deal of debate about the inclusion of women amid this august group.

Of the three criteria for being named a Doctor of the Church, the third criterion of producing "eminent doctrine" has been the most problematic. What does this term mean? For most of history, it has meant that the individual produced a sizable body of written work that influenced the universal Church in a positive way and responded to the needs of the contemporary Church. But if this criterion of a significant and coherent body of work is taken literally, many named Doctors of the Church do not qualify.

One factor in favor of the inclusion of figures who do not have a large written theological corpus is a broader, more inclusive understanding of theology. Realizing that theology takes diverse forms has brought about a new consciousness that recognizes the legitimacy and truth of the theological thought of persons who had been excluded for much of Christian history—including our four women Doctors of the Church. In all types of theology, the legacies of Doctors of the Church must make a creative contribution to doctrine, exhibit the mark of excellence, have a lasting influence, be faithful to the Gospel, and enhance the overall life of the Body of Christ. In these ways, their lives and writings are marked by the power and energy of the Holy Spirit.

The last forty years have witnessed an amazing resurgence of interest in Christian women authors—books and articles at both the scholarly and popular levels, inexpensive translations, films, and educational programs of every stripe. Most people are drawn to these women for their spiritualities, as many of them are known as mystics. But scholars are also acknowledging that some of these women should be recognized as preachers, philosophers, historians, exegetes, playwrights, poets, and theologians.

The modern practice of distinguishing between "academic" and "popular" religious writing legitimately points to issues of genre and style. But it does not follow that the former qualifies as theology and the latter does not. Both contain important theological content. That our understanding of theology is based largely on formal, academic treatises has resulted in excluding women from the theological conversation, marginalizing their theological ideas, and impoverishing the theological tradition as a whole. Indeed, the tradition is more rich and complex than we have been led to believe.

The women we are about to study explored a wide range of theological topics including Trinity, Christology, Holy Spirit, grace, the cross, Christian anthropology, the virtues, and the cosmos. They were women of prayer and women of action—offering a prophetic word to a world and Church ever in need of renewal and reform.[4] As Ellen Charry notes, "To be unfamiliar with women's writings is now to be theologically ill-educated."[5] This female theological legacy is enhanced by the wise decision of the Roman Catholic Church to canonize and name as Doctors of the Church Catherine of Siena (1970), Teresa of Avila (1970), Thérèse of Lisieux (1997) and Hildegard of Bingen (2012).

Women have been a vital part of the Christian community from the days of Mary of Nazareth, Mary Magdalene, Phoebe (Romans 16:1–2); Mary and Martha (Luke 10:38–42); Mary, the mother of John (Acts 12:12; Colossians 4:10); Lydia (Acts 16:14–15); Priscilla (Acts 18:4, 25–26); Lois and Eunice (2 Timothy 1:5); and Tabitha/Dorcas (Acts 9:36–43). There is no doubt that the Christian community has valued and honored women throughout its history. But more often, the history of the human race and of religion in particular has been a story about the devaluation and marginalization of women.

In most cultures, the norm for what it means to be human has been men. Women are judged to fall short of this norm—they are too emotional, not intellectually gifted, not spiritual enough to speak or teach about God, not meant to be seen or heard in public spaces. Women are possessions of men rather than free agents in their own right, endowed by God with equal freedom and dignity.

This bias against women remains with us in spite of extraordinary advances in the last two hundred years. We owe a debt of gratitude to those women and men who have worked to raise up women, to hunt for their presence in the historical record and to make this evidence available to a wide public. It strikes us as odd that it took the Church until the twentieth century to recognize officially the theological gifts of Christian women. The good news is that the four female Doctors of the Church represent but a fraction of the theologies written by women over the history of Christianity. There is much work left to be done to learn about, appreciate, and absorb the experience of God from women's perspectives.

Why Study the Past?

As Christians, we are part of a large, holy, and sinful community that reaches back to our Jewish ancestors and forward through the two-thousand-year history of Christianity. The unifying ground of this community is the rich and diverse experience of God in Christ and through the Holy Spirit. It is a gift to become more deeply aware of the scope of this community to which we belong. Its forms are many— family, friends, local parish, national, and global Church. The cloud of witnesses to Jesus Christ also includes Jews who knew and followed Jesus, and all those who chose to assent to the Good News of the Gospel as the stories of Jesus were told and written down, and the community began to worship God in his name. An ever-deepening awareness of this long and complex history saves us from being locked into narrow views that perceive reality only in terms of the present.

As we come to know these four women Doctors of the Church, we are invited to an intellectual, theological awakening, but also to a felt sense of presence and solidarity with these women and all women who have preceded us in the faith. To learn their stories and read their writings is to encounter them as sisters in the way that Mary and Elizabeth expressed their sisterhood in mutual presence and embrace. As in all good friendships, there is a time for sharing our stories and a time to engage in attentive listening—putting aside our preoccupations and viewpoints in order to focus on how these women wrote about their experience of God. Such a stance requires discipline and an open curious mind and heart. Who were these women? What kind of a world did they live in? What influenced their thought? What social forces helped or hindered their journey toward union with God and love of the world?

When we do history, there are two paths we do not want to take. The first looks at history as old, irrelevant, backward, and not worth our time. This may save us some time, but it ignores the truth that who we are now is dependent on the past in both conscious and unconscious ways. Without the past, there would not be this particular present. It also means that we live in a small world, limited to the last century or year or month. If you belonged to this group, you would not likely be reading this book. A second path to avoid is one in which the past is seen as perfect and automatically endowed with value simply because it is old. Adherents to this view are consumed with the untenable idea that there was such a thing as the good old days. When you look more closely at the facts of history, you realize that the past was filled with marvelous and horrible things—just like today.

A third caution involves the tendency to project our ideas and values onto the past. If we don't know very much about a given period in history, we are more likely to fill that void with contemporary values and needs. For example, the term *feminist* originated in the nineteenth century, so it would not be appropriate to call someone from the seventh century a feminist, even if she or he did or said something to support women's dignity and equality. It is not a good idea to go looking for evidence to back up our current concerns or complaints about the world or the Church. If we manage to avoid these three pitfalls, what can we say about helpful, productive ways to explore the past?

One challenge is to keep in tension two ideas: Our time is markedly different from times past, and yet as human beings we share areas of common ground. Let us use Catherine of Siena as an example. Realizing that we cannot experience directly what it was like to be a female living in Siena, Italy, in the fourteenth century allows us to become genuinely curious about what scholars have discovered about this era. This process involves the study of history—social, economic, intellectual, ecclesiastical, artistic. It also means learning about theological trends and to what ideas Catherine was likely to have been exposed.

Second, we need to pay very close attention to her texts. We don't want to overlook or edit out things that strike us as strange or even repulsive—and there are many things about medieval culture that appear odd and puzzling to twenty-first-century readers. Instead we ask: What does Catherine actually say? How does she organize her thoughts? What imagery does she use? What are her favorite Bible passages? The aim is not to ignore, camouflage, or obliterate the unique personalities and insights of these women.

Finally, we use our imaginations to cross over and imagine what it might have been like to be and think like Catherine of Siena. As students of the Tradition, we are called upon to be generous and humble in our interpretations and conclusions about her theology and spiritual life.

History is filled with "classic" texts that we interrogate, but as believers who trust that the Holy Spirit has been at work in the Church, we allow the texts to interrogate us. How can Catherine's theology shape our own and help us to grow as disciples of Christ?

Such openness is complemented by a healthy skepticism. We need not be afraid to ask hard questions about the sin and evil of the period, or about the ways in which Catherine might have been blinded or co-opted by the forces around her. The very otherness of history wakes us up and keeps us alert to ways of thinking about God that we may have never imagined. These women have the potential to both affirm and challenge their readers.

But the otherness of history is not the entire story. We can identify with these women on many fronts. They were human beings with intellect and emotion. They came from families. They laughed and knew joy. They became ill. They bled when pricked with a thorn. They cried when they lost loved ones. They were believers who desired a closer relationship with God. They ran into obstacles within themselves and in the world around them. They read and listened to the Scriptures. They succeeded and they failed. And they were deeply committed to love and serve those around them. These women may have been a lot smarter than we are, but that does not efface the great human and faith-filled ground we share with them.

As students of history, we begin with our experience, our questions, our longings, and our anxieties. For example:

- Do I think of the human person primarily as graced and made in the image and likeness of God, or primarily as sinful, unable to say yes to God's loving invitation to holiness?

- What are my favored images for God? Is God an intimate friend, someone who is always there in time of need or a generous, powerful Creator of our complex and beautiful universe? Is God a judge watching over my shoulder?

- I am not happy with the way I pray. I want to make some changes, but am not sure how to go about it.

- How do I think about the Holy Spirit and how does the Spirit function in my life?
- Is my faith grounded primarily in myself as an individual, or are the wellsprings of my faith fed by the community?
- Do I think of my faith and God in terms of gender? How do I see myself as a woman or man in the Church? Who are my models of holiness and of theological reflection? Do I see myself as a theologian?
- There is so much evil and suffering in the world that I am not sure who God is anymore or whether God is present to the world.

Then we move to the evidence and listen attentively to what the past is saying on its own terms. For example:

- How does this text talk about God? What kind of language is used? What imagery and metaphors show up in talk about God? Who plays the lead—the Father/Mother, the Son, or the Holy Spirit?
- What are some of the favorite Bible passages that show up frequently in this text? What does this tell us about the author's theology?
- What are the authors' favorite virtues? How do they talk about growing in virtue?
- Is there a big emphasis on self-sacrifice?
- How does the author see the dynamic between individual spirituality and the Body of Christ?

Finally we move back to the present to ask critical questions about what of this tradition can profitably be brought forward and what should be left behind as irrelevant or even dangerous for our own time. For example:

- What do I think are the most pressing spiritual needs of the moment? Do these texts address them in any way?
- In what ways does this text inspire me to love God more?
- How does this text wake me up intellectually, emotionally, and spiritually and broaden my ideas about God and the world?

- Are there specific theological ideas or spiritual practices that appeal to me to enhance my own spiritual journey?
- What are the things that should not be brought forward into our own time?
- What new questions emerge that I might pursue in my life of faith?

History is our past. We mine its follies and riches with hope and expectation that it can lead us to deeper faith and love, to greater Christian maturity, and to a more informed and life-giving theology. We uncover the Christian story to get a better idea of who we are (both good and bad) and who we want to be as Christians in the twenty-first century.[6]

What Is Theology?

What happens when you hear the word *theology*? For many, it is an esoteric term pointing to complicated, often boring texts that are beyond our reach as Christians. But—important as it is—formal, academic theology is not the only kind of theology. If we think of theology as making sense of God, it is an endeavor open to all the baptized.[7] Prayerful reflection on reality (including everyday life) in the light of my faith is a legitimate form of theology. The poor in base Christian communities, reflecting on their plight and finding solutions in light of the Gospel, is a form of theology. Being curious and asking questions about my faith is a way to do theology. Attending a lecture on theology, joining a Bible study group, reading a book about God—all of these are ways to do theology. It is good for the Church and the world if a wide range of different kinds of believers engage in the task of theology. We are a richer, fuller, more truthful Church because we honor the four women Doctors of the Church as theologians and take the time to learn from and reflect on their words.

Our understanding of God is not a permanent accomplishment located in the clouds. Theology is a living, breathing, evolving thing that views the Bible and Tradition in light of the joys, sorrows, and pressing needs of each generation. The questions, viewpoints, and insights of Augustine in fourth-century North Africa are not those of Julian of Norwich in fourteenth-century England, nor those of an aunt in Chicago who teaches chemistry and is the mother of three children. Things change for worse and for better. At the beginning, the Church was poor, and now it seems to prefer the trappings of wealth. For centuries, Christians taught that God approved of slavery, but no longer do so.

However, there are basic core truths that have stood the test of time: that God is a Trinity; that Jesus Christ is fully God and fully human; that the human person is created in the image and likeness of God; that the Holy Spirit empowers us to witness to the divine presence in the world through history; that the Bible is the inspired word of God. But as soon as we ask for specific categories, language, and interpretations through which we experience, understand, and express these truths, we are led into the particular circumstances of our present context. For example, the constant advance of science and the communications revolution influence the questions we ask and how we think about God. We are Christians now and our faith is influenced by what is going on around us. Thus theology has both universal and local dimensions to it.

Since the four women Doctors of the Church were female and also did not have access to formal theological education, they can be models for a much wider segment of the community. Many who are reading this book are already doing theology in a conscious way. Others are doing theology but do not realize it because of the way they define theology. Still others will be invited to engage in theology for the first time and begin to understand what this means for their lives as Christians.

There are many good definitions of theology. Some of the key elements might include the following. To stand before the world and take awe-filled notice of God's grandeur is the basic foundation of theology. Mark McIntosh speaks of it as sidling up to the mysteries of the cosmos and peering into their depths. Examples might include the toes and fingers of a newborn; the Grand Canyon or Mount Everest; or the tiniest gesture of tender love—seeing in these phenomena an invitation to share in the very mystery of Trinitarian life—God as Creator and participant in the destiny of the human race.[8]

Theology is faith seeking understanding (*fides quaerens intellectum*). It steps back from our experience of God and asks questions about its content and meaning. It identifies language with which to speak of God. Theology is ordered reflection. It relies on reason and logic but is not devoid of emotion. In prayerful and intelligent ways it creates categories through which we can name and encounter God. Theology relies on Tradition but also seeks creative innovations that will allow the theological past to speak in meaningful and challenging ways to the present. A brief glance at the table of contents of Thomas Aquinas's *Summa Theologiae* provides a snapshot of the breadth and depth of theological language and categories.

On the lookout for the Word of God in the world, theologians regard the world with a long, loving gaze, mimicking the way God faces creation, seeking the truth within the fabric of existence. Theology is about ultimate meaning—not the proximate meaning, for example, of biology or sociology. Theology asks about the meaning of everything in the long run—Who am I? Why am I on this earth? How do I treat others? What is love? What is the meaning of suffering? What is death? Over the centuries, Christians have done different kinds of theology in many different contexts.

Yet, in our time, it seems that few consider doing theology their business. This means either that we do not understand what theology is or we don't feel implicated in sorting out the truth of the Gospel. Surely plumbing the ultimate truth of our existence is interesting, and if so, then it is worth talking about, thinking about, and seeking to understand—"from the questions of the child to the adult's cry of agony before the darkness of the world; from the meticulous explorations of the scholar to the poet's refreshment of narrative and imagery worn too smooth with casual use."[9]

Types of Theology

There is a wide range of specializations in the study of theology. One might focus on the Bible or on a specific period in history—patristic, medieval, modern, or postmodern. Theology might concern itself with a particular topic, such as ethics, Christology, or Christian anthropology. There are also distinctions among different styles and methods of theology. In her book, *God and the Goddesses: Vision, Poetry, and Belief in the Middle Ages*, Barbara Newman summarizes these various types of theology.[10] You may be familiar with the term scholastic theology, a name given to the theology taught in the great medieval universities, and for a long time viewed as the only type of theology. It set the tone for later theologies that rely heavily on reason and take a systematic and scientific approach. Theology done outside the walls of the medieval university by monks was acknowledged as monastic theology. This type of theology emerges out of personal and communal prayer and reflection on the scriptures. It is formative and inspirational in its orientation.

A third type of theology was given impetus by the Fourth Lateran Council in 1215, a council that was concerned, among other things, with the education of the laity. This type is called pastoral theology, which is didactic in form, appearing in sermons, catechisms, prayer and meditation, confessors' manuals, and saints' lives. In the fourteenth century, another type of theology was named mystical or ascetical and was distinguished from the systematic theology of the schools. This theology might be described as unitive, ascetic, or erotic.

More recently, Bernard McGinn has identified what he calls "vernacular theology," whose practitioners include a preponderance of women who write in their native tongues rather than Latin. Genres might include visions, spiritual diaries, courtly dialogues, lyric poems, letters, or homilies.[11] Newman adds a sixth type of theology, which she calls imaginative theology. This type of theology employs the imagination in poetic and realistic ways. A well-known example of imaginative theology is Ignatius of Loyola's Spiritual Exercises, in which the retreatant is asked to extend the stories of the Bible in creative, imaginative ways. It asks that we place ourselves directly into the setting of the meditation, e.g., the birth of Jesus, and imagine the details of the surroundings such as color, temperature, dialog, and emotions.

There is overlap among these different types of theology. Monastic, vernacular, mystical, and imaginative theologies make primary use of symbols, images, and metaphors. But this does not mean that you will never find a metaphor in scholastic theological writing. An individual author might produce theology from more than one of these types during his or her lifetime. Thomas Aquinas is famous for his rational, philosophical approach to theology, but he also wrote several beautiful Eucharistic hymns such as the *Pange Lingua*.

While Hildegard wrote in Latin, Catherine and Teresa wrote in their local dialects. The style of their texts is more poetic and symbolic than linear, grounded not in the language of the university, but in that of the Bible, liturgy, divine office, and *lectio divina* in which these women were immersed. Many female mystics writing in the vernacular engage in a more fluid, intuitive, associative interpretation of the Bible. Often their metaphors seem foreign to us because they arise from a time and place that is dramatically different from our own. For example, Catherine speaks of the Trinity in these terms: the Father is the table; the Son is the food on the table; the Holy Spirit is the waiter who serves at the table— images that come from Catherine's personal experience of waiting on table in her home. These metaphors were also no doubt influenced by the images the women saw in religious art and heard in sacred music. In addition, the texts are filled with paradox as they struggle to capture their experience of mystical encounter and union with God—experiences that go well beyond the capability of both ordinary and poetic language.

Even though there are differences in the modes and styles of these various types of theology, it is important to remember that they all share the goals of deepening the community's understanding of the faith and moving the reader to deeper holiness and love of neighbor. No matter the style, authentic theology provides distinctive teaching about theological realities such as God, creation, the human person, the fall, salvation history, and the relationship between God and the soul.

WOMEN AS THEOLOGIANS

We are privileged to live in an age in which the term "woman theologian" is no longer an oxymoron. But the age-old stereotype of women as weak, hysterical, and unable to learn or to lead dies hard. For much of its history, the Roman Church has banned women from teaching in public about God or studying theology, and it continues to ban them from ordained leadership and most decision making. Women's intellectual gifts were blocked, ignored and ridiculed for centuries. While enormous strides have been made in some parts of the world, women continue to face enormous obstacles in many countries around the globe.[12] The consequences of this negative stereotype include a host of treatises not written; poetry not expressed; classes not taught; sermons not delivered; biblical texts not interpreted; music not composed; witness not given—a huge loss to the Church and to the world.

That, for most of history, women were not allowed to enroll in institutions of higher education had a number of consequences. They did not have the formal credentials, the language or the office to participate in ecclesial reflection or decision-making. Lack of education also disempowered women from being informed or making decisions about their own lives. This does not mean that women were theologically illiterate. It does not take much exposure to their texts to discover how intelligent, even brilliant they are. They put their God-given minds to work on whatever information they had. This included conversations with educated clerics; access to books; listening to sermons and lectures; participating in the divine office and reading and hearing the Scriptures in many different settings.

When courageous, prophetic women did choose to speak out, they inevitably raised issues of authority. In general, theological authority was based on office (monks or clerics) or in education. Women had neither. Instead, alternate sources of empowerment were acknowledged, the primary being experience and witness to holiness linked to the Holy Spirit. The negative consequences of a decision to write and preach theology in the public sphere are not surprising.

We can document a great deal of opposition, refusal, ridicule and censure on the part of those in power within and beyond the Church. Evaluative and punitive measures were put in place that ranged from verbal censure to the Inquisition, whose judgments might include torture and death. In most cases, early women theologians survived and their writings were preserved because of their intelligence, courage, creativity and perseverance. Many also depended on male supporters in the halls of power who were able to advocate for them, argue that the Church should affirm them, and offer editorial counsel and strategies to the women themselves.

The presence of women's theological voices also engendered a new awareness of the important role of the Holy Spirit in the Church and the need for discernment. In order to defend the orthodoxy of theology written by women, appeal was consistently made to the Holy Spirit. In each case, judgment had to be made as to whether the experience of divine encounter recorded by these women was authentic or heretical. The process of such discernment was complex. Considerations included the woman's identity and character; her lifestyle and behavior; her male support; the needs of the Church; her witness to the Gospel. We can be grateful for ecclesiastical decisions that supported the preservation of the texts we discuss here. We also know that mistakes were made (for men as well) and legitimate writing and its authors were banned, banished, and burned.

The emergence of large numbers of women theologians in the thirteenth century changed the game of theology in significant ways. The use of the vernacular, along with less expensive ways to make paper, greatly enlarged the ranks of authors and especially of readers. All the gains women made can be applied equally to the more affluent, educated laity. Instead of theology being the exclusive preserve of monks and clerics, it was now available in fresh forms to large segments of the

Church. For the first time since the early Church, there was a greater variety of participants in the theological conversation. The turn to the vernacular leveled the playing field in ways hard for us in the twenty-first century to imagine.

Readers today benefit greatly from this creative theology, which is often different from mainline theology written by men. In notable ways, these women theologians made creative use of traditional metaphors but also invented fresh, new images that are not part of the mainline tradition. Without the established, recognized categories of theology that come with formal education, women were forced to rely on their own experience, to work in new ways with ideas, metaphors, and images, and to create a type of theology in their own key. Hildegard portrays the Church and charity as powerful female figures. Catherine of Siena assigns to the Holy Spirit the role of holding the nails in Christ's hands and feet secure. Thérèse of Lisieux and Catherine speak of God's hunger and thirst for souls. Teresa's famous image of the butterfly has enriched and guided spiritual pilgrims since the sixteenth century.

These four women teach us how to integrate passionate love of God and world with intellectual work. Thérèse consciously rejected dependence on theological and spiritual authors, grounding her theology in practice. Because women were denied roles as professors or clergy, their theologies—while sophisticated in notable ways—have a home-grown flavor to them. Their commitment to ministry, whether direct or through prayer, privileged theology's connection with service to the poor, the sick and those in trouble.

Hildegard was concerned with healing and Catherine, as a member of the Dominican Third Order called the Mantellate, brought food and a healing touch to the poor in her neighborhood. They functioned in many roles that combined theological and pastoral concerns. They were reformers, ethicists, and activists as well as theologians. They were in touch with the failure, suffering, illness, corruption, sinfulness, and oppression that surrounded them and brought forth their theologies from these pressing human needs with empathy and compassion. Like feminist theology today, a primary aim of their theology was practical. They wanted to move Church and society to accountability, humanness, justice, virtue, and peace.

In addition to learning from their environment, women were empowered to engage in what we might call creative bypasses. By this I mean innovative alternatives that refused to let a closed door shut down their choice to speak. The risks involved for women speaking or writing for a public audience beyond their monasteries were significant. They had to have a bold and courageous spirit. This may be hard for us to understand since we live in an age in which anyone is free to express themselves in any way they wish—with few consequences. In contrast, medieval women could be imprisoned, tortured, or burned at the stake for transgressing established gender barriers of Church and society.

For women, the power to speak about God had many sources, human and divine. These women were from aristocratic or affluent merchant classes, which often meant that they had access to rudimentary education—at home or at a local convent or school. They were also connected to leaders in many sectors of society from popes to emperors. Each had a call to engage in a profound relationship with God that she took seriously and pursued with determination and commitment. This usually meant that they did not marry, but entered some form of religious life that afforded them more time and space to reflect, pray and write. It would have been impossible for them to thrive unless society and Church believed that God spoke through them. If judged authentic, these holy women were welcomed, honored, and even sought after for their gifts of theological insight and prophecy.

Medieval anthropology held that female vulnerability made it easy for the devil to tempt and beguile them (the story of Eve is paradigmatic here) but this same vulnerability made women more available to spiritual contact with God, angels, and saints—the Annunciation and Magnificat provided models. The biblical preference for the poor and lowly as instruments of God's word set the stage for the reception by the Church of women's theological voices.

It is also clear that the Church needed these voices. The lives and writings of all four women responded to specific crises in the Church—some during their lifetimes, others after they died. Catherine was called upon to address the problems associated with the Avignon popes who had left Rome to live in France. Teresa of Avila engineered the Carmelite reform in Spain in the aftermath of the Protestant Reformation. Hildegard spoke out forcefully against the growing popularity of the Cathars who were seen as deviating from the doctrine of the Church. After her death, Thérèse of Lisieux was seen as instrumental in protecting France from the encroachment of England that threatened French national identity —a situation in which the Church was deeply enmeshed.

Given the persistent exclusion of women from theology across the centuries, it is a pleasure and a privilege to be able to read their texts and reflect on the theological insights of these four women Doctors of the Church. They function as rare female guides who teach us to take discipleship seriously and embrace the baptismal calling and responsibility to think theologically. They are our sisters in the faith, women of courage who had the creativity and the stamina to talk and write about God. Their theologies are all the more precious for being minority reports— saving us from an exclusively male theological perspective. They invite us to cast our eyes back into history and also forward as we continue to build on their legacy, bringing women's voices to the theological task in ever-greater numbers and from ever distant shores.

Focus of This Book

Since it is impossible in the space of one short book to present a comprehensive overview of the theologies of these four women Doctors of the Church, I have chosen one specific theological focus for each woman: Hildegard's theology of the Holy Spirit; Catherine's theology of incarnation; Teresa's theology of grace; and Thérèse of Lisieux's theology of the cross.

The order is chronological. We begin with Hildegard of Bingen (1098–1179), who is the most recent woman to be named a Doctor of the Church (2012), then we discuss Catherine of Siena (1347–1380), Teresa of Avila (1515–1582), and Thérèse of Lisieux (1873–1897). Within a Church that has worked to uphold the dignity of women stands a Church with a history of ambivalence, anxiety, and failure toward women. And yet, we are here today reflecting—albeit belatedly—on the theologies of four women who have been named doctors of the universal Church.

THEOLOGICAL REFLECTION

- What is it that draws you most strongly to women's theological texts?
- What do you think are the most pressing theological/spiritual needs of the moment? What do women theologians have to offer?
- Who is God for you? Identify one or two images or metaphors that capture best who God is in your life.
- Do you think of your faith and God in terms of gender? How do you see yourself as a woman or man in the church? Who are your models of holiness?
- Do you see yourself as a theologian?

CHAPTER TWO

Hildegard of Bingen (1098–1179)
Theology of the Holy Spirit

H ildegard is rightly called a Renaissance woman—even though she lived long before the period that we now know as the Renaissance. The breadth and depth of her productivity would be amazing in any century, and is especially so in the twelfth. Barbara Newman, the leading Hildegard scholar in the United States, wonderfully captures the range of Hildegard's erudition:

> Hildegard was the only woman of her age to be accepted as an authoritative voice on Christian doctrine; the first woman who received express permission from a pope to write theological books; the only medieval woman who preached openly, before mixed audiences of clergy and laity, with the full approval of church authorities; the author of the first known morality play and the only twelfth-century playwright who is not anonymous; the only composer of her era (not to mention the only medieval woman) known both by name and by a large corpus of surviving music; the first scientific writer to discuss sexuality and gynecology from a female perspective; and the first saint whose official biography included a first-person account.[1]

The question discussed in chapter one about whether women had the requisite body of written theological work to be named a Doctor of the Church clearly does not apply to Hildegard.

Hildegard—and the other women we will study—is both a woman of her time and a woman whose theology transcends time and place, speaking to later generations. There are aspects of her thought that made sense in the twelfth century but are no longer relevant today. For example, she employed sexual metaphors for the spiritual life and openly discussed sexuality from a medical perspective, but she had a certain disdain for physical sexual activity. In addition, some of her healing techniques, while state of the art in the twelfth century, appear to us as magical and superstitious. Coming from an aristocratic background, Hildegard seems elitist in some of her attitudes about religious life, ideas that clash with a more egalitarian, democratic outlook. However, our focus is on those aspects of her theology, imagery and symbolism that are most likely to reverberate with our time and place—luring us to become fuller human beings, made in God's image and called to a creative and courageous life of Gospel love.

Benedict XVI welcomed Hildegard into the community of official saints on May 10, 2012, and named her a Doctor of the Church on October 7 of that year. In 1979, the nuns of Eibingen and the conference of German bishops had submitted proposals for her canonization. But the story goes back much further. The first petition for sainthood was addressed to Gregory IX in 1228, submitted by Hildegard's Rupertsberg nuns. But a confluence of events, bureaucratic bumbling, and time worked against it.

Locally, Hildegard has long been considered a saint. In 1940 Pius XII made September 17 her official feast day for all of Germany. Now she will be so honored by the universal Church. At the liturgy in which Hildegard and St. John of Avila were proclaimed Doctors of the Church, one of the prayers of the faithful called on the Holy Spirit in the context of Hildegard's many gifts: "for people dedicated to culture, science and medicine": "May the Holy Spirit, through the intercession of St. Hildegard of Bingen, strengthen in us the will to do good and to hold goodness and beauty dear, so that people may glorify God and learn to advance the dignity of every person."[2]

Life and Works

Hildegard, the last of ten children, was born in 1098 into a noble family to Hildebert of Bermersheim and his wife, Mechthild, in the lush green valley of the Rhine.[3] When Jutta of Sponheim, the young daughter of a local highborn family, decided to enter religious life as a teenager, Hildegard's parents offered Hildegard as her companion—a "tithe to God." Hildegard was eight years old. Such a custom appears alarming to us, but in the twelfth century, a surge of religious enthusiasm motivated many, even the very young, to give up marriage and possessions and go apart to live a life of solitude and self-sacrifice. Three of Hildegard's siblings also followed vocations in the Church—one brother became a cantor at the Cathedral in Mainz; another was a canon in Tholey, and a sister became a nun at Hildegard's monastery. At first, Jutta and Hildegard lived together in the home of a widow in the area. When Jutta was twenty and Hildegard fourteen, they went to the monastery of St. Disibod and took monastic vows as recluses—enclosed in a cell and cut off from the world.[4]

Hildegard would have learned enough Latin to chant the psalms, but her command of the language remained rough. Her writing does not reflect the level of polish and sophistication of works written by her contemporary in France, the wealthy, well-educated Héloise. Nonetheless, this did not stop Hildegard from producing a significant theological corpus.

Although the foundation of the holy site of St. Disibod went back to the seventh century, it had long been abandoned and was only recently being rebuilt when Hildegard arrived. Hildegard's many architectural references stem from being surrounded by construction during her early years at the monastery. Building was also part of her life later when she founded her own convent in Rupertsberg. In 1136, in part due to her extreme ascetic practices, Jutta died at the young age of forty-four. Hildegard was elected prioress of the small group of ten women at St. Disibod.

Hildegard reported that from an early age, while wide awake, she saw images in living color—what she called the "shadow of the Living Light." These images included buildings, shimmering light, larger-than-life female figures such as Caritas and Ecclesia, umbilical cords, cosmic eggs, and mountains. On occasion, she reported that she had a direct divine encounter with the "Living Light" itself. Scholars discuss Hildegard's openness to the divine and her prophetic spirit in tandem with a recent hypothesis that she may have suffered from severe migraine headaches. The visions Hildegard described resemble reports from patients with migraine, e.g., starbursts in their peripheral vision. Hypothesizing about a medical diagnosis is helpful in our quest to know Hildegard, but it need not jeopardize the ways in which Hildegard and the entire Church gradually understood her visions as part of her call from God to become theologian and prophet.

In 1141 at the age of forty-three, Hildegard heard a voice telling her to write down what she was experiencing. The trauma induced at the thought of writing—there was no precedent for public female theologians—made her sick. It was only her choice to risk writing that made her whole again. When she wrote to the then popular Bernard of Clairvaux to ask him what he thought about her visions, she received an affirming, albeit cautious response. In turn, Bernard presented some of her work to Pope Eugene III at a Church synod in Trier in 1147. Hildegard received the approbation of the papacy, which made her a celebrity, allowing her to write and preach widely in Germany. Hildegard's visions, prophetic insight, and reputation as a healer drew crowds on pilgrimage from across the region, bringing fame, blessings and money to the monastery.

The reasons for such an unusual papal blessing are complex. But one motivation was surely the Church's need to fight the growing attraction of reforming groups such as the Cathars who taught a dualistic doctrine that the Church considered heretical. The Cathar movement arose in response to the laxity and greed of clergy and the lack of spiritual rigor among the faithful. Many Christians, including many women, were attracted to reforming groups that offered a more rigorous, virtue-oriented way of life.

The Cathars questioned the value of the sacraments and viewed the material world as the evil creation of an evil god. Hildegard must have known about the Cathars, some of whom were burned at the stake in Cologne in 1163. Some of Hildegard's theology is aimed at correcting these non-orthodox viewpoints.

In 1148, Hildegard received another message from God, ordering her to leave St. Disibod and establish her own monastery. We can only conjecture the practical reasons for such a move. Perhaps the nuns' quarters were not conducive to their life of prayer and study. Perhaps Hildegard chafed at the oversight of the male Abbot or the lack of control over the land and financial endowments brought to the monastery by her sisters—all from wealthy families. In any event, the decision caused great consternation in Abbot Kuno, head of Disibod, and among the sisters who were not at all sure they wanted to take on a life of poverty and hardship that building a new monastery would entail. Hildegard became gravely ill, and eventually the Abbot agreed to let her go after she denounced him as working against the will of God. Hildegard's reputation for holiness and her approval by the Church meant that everyone took her seriously, for her words and desires were thought to be rooted in the will of God.

Still, Hildegard had to pay a hefty sum to the monks to win release. With the help of wealthy patrons such as Archbishop Henry of Mainz and the marchioness Richardis of Stade, Hildegard purchased the land and in 1150 began to build a new monastery on Mount St. Rupert, or Rupertsberg. By the end of her life, at eighty-one years, the monastery housed about fifty nuns. Her monastery had grown so large by the 1160s that she founded a second monastery across the Rhine in Eibingen, which remains a functioning religious community and a center for Hildegard research.

In 1158, at the age of sixty, Hildegard engaged in four preaching tours in Germany and Swabia, bringing her reforming message to monks, clergy, and laity. In 1173, Hildegard wrote of her sorrow when her beloved friend and secretary, Volmar, died. He was replaced in 1177 by the monk Guibert of Gembloux, whose support of Hildegard went back to her early days as a Benedictine nun.

There is a story about Hildegard's final clash with the Church. Near the very end of her life in 1178–1179, she had buried a nobleman in her monastic cemetery. The bishop contested this burial, claiming that the man had not died in a state of grace. Hildegard protested that he had given a death bed confession that made him eligible for burial in sacred ground, and she obscured the burial site so that no one could disinter the body.

The actual facts of the case and Hildegard's motivation are likely permanently lost in the sands of history. This man was of a noble family and Hildegard was consistently supportive of this class, to which she herself belonged. We are certain about one outcome of her determined opposition to the wishes of the bishop. He placed an interdict on her monastery forbidding the nuns to celebrate liturgy and the Divine Office. In response, Hildegard issued a harsh warning to the bishops to think twice before making a decision to silence the praise of God.

Hildegard was a prolific writer. She was assisted by secretaries—her dear friend, the monk Volmar, and a sister very dear to her, Richardis of Stade. To enhance the reputation of her monastery's patron, Hildegard wrote the *Life of St. Rupert* as well as a liturgical sequence and series of antiphons to be sung on his feast day. In all, she wrote some seventy liturgical songs compiled as the *Symphony of the Harmony of Celestial Revelations*. Her theological works include a trilogy: *Know the Ways of the Lord/Scivias* (1141–1151); the *Book of Life's Merits/Liber vitae meritorum* (1158–1163) and the *Book of Divine Works/Liber divinorum operum* (1163–1173). A visual thinker, Hildegard's texts need to be read in tandem with her images, which form an integral part of her theology.

In the first volume, *Scivias*, Hildegard presents a panoramic theological treatment of salvation history from creation to the eschaton. She treats creation, the fall, the Trinity, the Church and sacraments, and the last judgment. She views history as a monumental spiritual battle between the forces of good and evil. Thus, personified virtues play a major role in her description of the Christian life—Patience, Charity, Chastity, Prudence. In the second volume, Hildegard portrays the vices that conspire to deter Christians from the path of virtue. This text resembles manuals instructing clergy how to ask questions during confession and suggesting appropriate penances. Hildegard's text also urges lay people to atone for their sins through fasting and giving to the poor. To motivate her readers, Hildegard paints a rather dire and scary portrait of the torments of purgatory.

In the third volume, the *Book of Divine Works,* Hildegard explores the harmonies in creation between the macrocosm of the cosmos and the microcosm of the human person, which mirror each other. Her image of a male body affixed on a circular background representing the universe provides a visual image of the world inscribed in the human body.[5] Further evidence of this correspondence is visible in the homilies she preached to her sisters. In the *Book of Divine Works* she explores the divine fiery life that permeates sun, moon, waters, and stars. God is not so much an omnipotent Creator removed from creation, as the very life force within it. Humanity holds a place of honor within the cosmos, having been made in the image and likeness of God. She then moves from cosmology to history and the relationships between past, present, and future. She offers trenchant criticisms of the Church and prophecies about the end of the world.

Hildegard also wrote about medicine. In the Middle Ages most medical care was provided by monasteries. Hoping for both physical and spiritual cures, pilgrims visited holy sites, which often contained a hospice for the sick poor.[6] In this milieu, Hildegard's interest in medicinal herbs and cures would flower. Her medical treatises include the *Book of Simple Medicine* and the *Book of Compound Medicine* (also known as

Causes and Cures). She also composed the *Play of Virtues/Ordo virtutum* in which the major virtues are personified, locked in a battle with the devil for a young soul. The only non-singing voice is the devil—life without God is a life that cannot "sing." We also have several hundred of Hildegard's letters.

Twelfth-Century Context

The twelfth century is often described as a renaissance. Europe witnessed urban growth; more and more land was being cultivated; the first Crusade was preached in 1099; scholarship and study of the Bible was becoming more sophisticated in the cathedral schools. New religious orders included the Cistercians, the Carthusians, and the Premonstratensians. This flowering of intellectual and spiritual curiosity paved the way for the founding of the great European universities in the thirteenth century.

Hildegard's contemporaries include Anselm of Canterbury, Bernard of Clairvaux, Abelard and Héloise, Hugh and Richard of St. Victor, Thomas à Becket, and Eleanor of Aquitaine. This creative ferment drew on the rediscovery of Greco-Roman culture, the theologies of the Eastern fathers of the Church, and encounters with Islam. New knowledge led to a reexamination of business as usual in all aspects of life and fostered optimism and a widespread desire to discover meaning in human history.

Old ways of viewing the relationship between the supernatural and natural worlds gave way to a new awareness of the integrity of nature. The world remained connected to God through creation and God's ongoing presence, but divine activity was seen more in terms of the workings of nature itself, rather than primarily through supernatural beings or movements that came from outside nature. The world was viewed as connected in all its parts—a great chain of being that emerged from God and, in the end, returned to the embrace of the Trinity.

Like the theory of evolution in our time, the theory of an ordered, hierarchical universe functioned as an overarching framework for the twelfth century. A sacramental view of the world prevailed in which the visible outer world symbolized a deeper, hidden truth. Hildegard was a woman of her time in her use of symbols, metaphors, analogies and allegories to speak about how the world revealed the sacred. Animals, nature, color, numbers, art, the human person, names—all of history contained hints of the divine.

Innovative, technological advances included the harnessing of water power to grind flour; hydraulic wheels that enabled one horse to do the work of twenty-five; windmills; new armaments; new means of transport; and the mechanical clock. Hildegard is an excellent example of twelfth-century curiosity about nature, the makeup and capabilities of the human person, and reflection on interior consciousness and motives.

Within the Church, there was growing concern about the lack of knowledge and spiritual maturity among the laity. The Fourth Lateran Council of 1215 emphasized the sacraments by mandating for the first time that all Christians were to go to confession to a priest and receive communion once a year. In other ways spirituality was newly extended to include laity, many of whom were drawn to a simple lifestyle, itinerant preaching, pilgrimage, crusades, and Gospel witness. Laity became dissatisfied with the worldliness of the Church and openly criticized it. Many joined reform movements such as the Waldensians, a group that began in Lyons, France in the 1170s, and the Humiliati, dating from the early twelfth century in Italy. Rather than begging, they supported simplicity of life through the work of their hands, advocated a vernacular Bible, and lay preaching. Biblical support was found in Mark 15:5, "Go out to the whole world and preach the Gospel to all creatures," and Acts 5:29, "One must obey God more than people." No doubt Hildegard was inspired by some of these same desires.

All these positive developments seem to clash with Hildegard's keen sense of ecclesial failings. The Church was struggling to carry forward the Carolingian reforms of the previous century. As prophet, Hildegard noticed, and was acutely disturbed by, monks who schemed to become priors because of the wealth and prestige attached to this office. She was disheartened by religious leaders who wrote to her because they had grown weary and wanted to opt out of leadership positions. She was impatient with lax monastic discipline and superiors who dealt with it in harsh and unloving ways. She made the Church the object of her extensive reforming efforts, speaking out against greed, dissent, and power struggles.

During this period, there was a sustained conflict over power. Nobles became a strong block often in conflict with the king and/or the papacy. The battle between secular rulers and the papacy was fierce and prolonged. Much was at stake. It is hard for us to imagine Church leaders competing for secular power with intrigue, armies, recriminations, excommunications, and more.

Bishops functioned as princes who worked for civil rulers and benefited from their rewards. One key aspect of the struggle was the question of who had the power to appoint bishops and assign them to dioceses. Since Constantine in the early fourth century, emperors had called councils and seen themselves as the primary protectors of the faith. In the Middle Ages, the papacy confronted the secular power of kings and rulers within the Church. The stakes were high—money, prestige, power, and control.

A compromise was worked out at the Concordat of Worms in 1122, but it did not hold, since the bishops remained conflicted between their political loyalty to the empire and ecclesiastical loyalty to the pope. Rhetoric and action deteriorated on both sides. When kings did not agree on the elected pope they simply appointed their own. Frederick Barbarossa was responsible for a schism that lasted from 1150 to 1177. Rejecting the elected pope, Alexander II, Frederick appointed his own popes—Victor IV, then Paschal III, and finally Calixtus III. While Hildegard was sympathetic to Barbarossa on many issues, she excoriated him for prolonging this division in the Church. In turn, popes declared allegiance to other kings when the king in question was not to their liking. Pope Gregory VII deposed King Henry IV in 1075. The army of Henry V attacked Rome. Hildegard viewed the greed, political intrigue, and self-interest of civil and ecclesiastical leaders in Germany as a cancer within the Church.

These conflicts made life uncertain. Political and family allegiances could shift quickly. One's fortunes could be booming one day and decimated the next. There was simultaneously great oppression in the name of religion and also significant religious enthusiasm and a taste for reform.

Hildegard's Theology of the Holy Spirit

Hildegard's theology of the Holy Spirit relies heavily on imagery from the Bible (such as that found in Isaiah 11:1–3; Psalm 103; Ecclesiasticus 24) and from nature: fire, breath/air/wind, oil, water, earth. Her theology reflects a keen sacramental consciousness—all of reality glows with the presence of God its Creator.[7] Also important to Hildegard is the Spirit's renewing, life-giving role in the sacraments of baptism and confirmation through water and chrism oil. Hildegard speaks of Pentecost and confirmation:

> The sweetness of the Holy Spirit is immeasurable and swift, encircling all creatures in grace…. Its path is a torrent…. For the Holy Spirit is a burning and shining serenity that will never be depleted and which kindles fiery virtues so that, by the Holy Spirit, all darkness is banished.[8]

When it comes to the divine presence, water and fire do not cancel each other out but work together to nurture virtue and goodness.

The Spirit also has a theological role in bringing forth and kindling true doctrine. Hildegard's theology of the Holy Spirit is best understood in the context of her theology of the Trinity. Unlike theology today, medieval theology was steeped in a lively, existential awareness of omnipresent Trinitarian patterns. Hildegard even structures her theological work in a threefold manner. She portrays the three persons interacting with each other and the world—prodding, demanding, consoling, and loving. While Christ plays a more central role in her theology, the Spirit is given much more than a walk-on part. In a wonderful description of the Trinity, Hildegard left us a rare example of a Christian theologian who expends more ink on the Spirit than on the first two persons.

> And so these three Persons are in the unity of inseparable substance; but They are not indistinct among themselves. How? He Who begets is the Father; He Who is born is the Son; and He Who in eager freshness proceeds from the Father and the Son, and sanctified the waters by moving over their face in the likeness of an innocent bird, and streamed with ardent heat over the apostles, is the Holy Spirit.[9]

Not only the Church, but also all of reality is seen as a visible, dynamic sacrament of the Trinity—unity through multiplicity.

> As the flame of a fire has three qualities, so there is one God in three Persons. How? A flame is made up of brilliant light and red power and fiery heat. It has brilliant light that it may shine, and red power that it may endure, and fiery heat that it may burn.[10]

In this description, the Spirit is the fiery heat who "burns ardently in the minds of the faithful." In an antiphon for the Trinity in her *Symphonia*, we witness Hildegard's sacramental view of the world. She hears God's harmonious presence in all of life.

> To the Trinity be praise!
>   God is music, God is life
>   that nurtures every creature in its kind.
>   Our God is the song of the angel throng
>   and the splendor of secret ways
>   hid from all humankind,
>   But God our life is the life of all.[1]

SPIRIT OF PROPHECY

The Spirit plays a central role in Hildegard's role as prophet—she was known as the "Sibyl of the Rhine." In her visions, she saw into present and future realities on earth and in heaven. We have noted that the primary authority of women theologians and mystics rested in their being inspired by the Holy Spirit. Hildegard, her religious community, and the wider Church understood her visions as a gift from the Spirit. In *Know the Ways of the Lord,* Hildegard hears God speak to her:

> But, O human, if you love Me, I embrace you, and I will warm you with the fire of the Holy Spirit. For when you contemplate Me with a good intention and know Me by your faith, I will be with you. But those who despise Me turn to the Devil, and choose not to know Me; and therefore I too reject them.[12]

In a letter to Bernard of Clairvaux, she described her visions as "great marvels" revealed by the Spirit of God. She used the Latin term *lux vivens* or "living light" to describe the dynamic presence within her that also penetrated every aspect of creation. The tradition has consistently named this ongoing divine presence in history, Holy Spirit. Hildegard's experience of Spirit is reminiscent of the New Testament accounts of the power of God that remained in the community after Jesus died and rose from the dead—dynamic, energetic, lively.

While it is unlikely that Hildegard had access to the ideas of her Italian contemporary Joachim of Fiore, his worldview gives insight into the world of the twelfth century and its intellectual and spiritual currents. Ideas about the end of time, known as apocalyptic, were grounded in the New Testament book of Revelation. Until Joachim, the future of the world was seen in dark and dramatic terms—a consuming fire, violent conflict, and the coming of the Antichrist (2 Thessalonians 2:7–12).

Joachim's innovation was to see the future in more positive terms. He viewed history in three broad periods. The first, from Adam to Christ, was identified with the first person of the Trinity and with married laity.

The second belonged to Christ (and secondarily to the Holy Spirit), was linked with clergy, and was to last about twelve hundred years. The third period belonged to the Holy Spirit, and was embodied in monasticism. Salvation history began with Elijah and St. Benedict, and would come to full flower sometime after the year 1200. He saw the final drama not as the end of history, but as its fulfillment when the Church would be reformed and enjoy a time of peace and contemplation. Hildegard writes of a five-stage history, but in her homilies, she simplifies the schema to three, reflecting her Trinitarian consciousness. She too links the final era to the Holy Spirit.

The Spirit is also present in Hildegard's constant use of the familiar Spirit metaphor of fire. She describes God as "a dazzling fire, totally alive." Within this fire is the flame of the Word who became incarnate through the "greenness" of the Holy Spirit. Hildegard is drawn into the story of Christ's birth, saying less about Christ's passion and death. As we have seen, Hildegard's theology focuses on human behavior and the connections between the human person and creation as well as the inner harmony of soul and body.

Spirit of Reform

Hildegard's ability to see into the future and preach a prophetic word to a sinful Church and society placed her within the prophetic tradition of Judaism and Christianity. Enlivened by the Spirit, she openly called kings and emperors to task for interfering with the Church and fueling division and conflict. But it took courage to voice her concern that the cancer of the Antichrist was not outside the Church but was coming forth from its very womb. It needed to be exorcised.[13] This is her graphic description of a corrupt Ecclesia:

> And you see again the figure of a woman...from the waist down.... And from her waist to the place that denotes the female, she has various scaly blemishes...a black and monstrous head. It has fiery eyes, and ears like an ass', and nostrils and

mouth like a lion's.... It opens wide its jowls and terribly clashes its horrible iron-colored teeth.[14]

Hildegard spoke against the buying and selling of Church offices (simony). She fought heresy and schism and chastised clergy who were living hypocritical, dissolute lives. Ironically, it seems as though her disillusionment about the possibility of reform propelled her to bolder and bolder demands for conversion.

She warned clergy and monks that they would be forcibly divested of all their wealth and position by secular powers. She envisioned a small remnant of faithful, devoted clergy living pure, dedicated lives as hermits. The Spirit's presence nurtured her hope for institutional reform. She wrote to the Cistercians of Eberbach:

> You therefore who fear God, hear the Spirit of the Lord saying to you: Rid yourselves of this wickedness, and cleanse yourselves so that henceforth you exercise more restraint than you have heretofore. Thus purify yourselves before the day of those tribulations when God's enemies, and yours, force you to flee into your proper place of humility and poverty.[15]

Hildegard identified with the author of the book of Revelation. Her goal was a return to the "first dawn of justice" when a purified and repentant clergy would usher in the peace and harmony of a new Pentecost. Relying on the Spirit, Hildegard broke new ground in her courage and willingness to confront both civil and ecclesiastical leaders with harsh but hopeful words. Her role as reformer embodies a theology of the Spirit that empowers humanity to be courageous and unafraid. It is a Spirit who gives her the words to confront ecclesial and political evil. It is a Spirit who can be trusted to bring about effective reform and renewal.

Chants of Praise

Singing the liturgy and the Divine Office was at the heart of Benedictine life.[16] Music was important to Hildegard in a personal way. Not only did she participate in the daily round of sung prayer, but she also composed new texts and melodies to enrich the liturgical life of her monastery.[17] It was common in Benedictine circles to link liturgical singing with the Holy Spirit. External rituals were intended to bring about interior Spirit power and transformation. Singing was carried by breath, a symbol long associated with the Holy Spirit. Caritas, the Spirit of love says, "For I am skilled in every breath of the Spirit of God, so I pour out the most limpid streams."[18]

For Hildegard, the idea of "harmony" referred not only to the music they sang, but had a broader theological significance. It pointed to the cosmic order of the celestial spheres, to the original right relationship between the divine and the human before the fall, as well as to paradise. It was also a primary means of creating harmony within a person, uniting physical, psychological, and spiritual dimensions. Liturgical chant was therefore, an important work of the Spirit, which was why Hildegard was so angry with the bishops who silenced their singing. She condemned this decision harshly because she saw such silencing as shutting down the Spirit's power and work in the world.

Hildegard composed two antiphons, a hymn and a sequence in honor of the Holy Spirit. For Hildegard the Spirit had a life-giving, healing, unitive effect on the world and on the individual person.

> The Spirit of God
> is a life that bestows life,
> root of the world-tree
> and wind in its boughs.
> Scrubbing out sins,
> she rubs oil into wounds.
> She is glistening life
> alluring all praise,
> all-awakening,
> all-resurrecting.[19]

In her hymn to the Holy Spirit, Hildegard relates the Sprit directly to music.

> Praise to you
> Spirit of fire!
> to you who sound the timbrel
> and the lyre.
> Your music sets our minds
> ablaze! The strength of our souls
> awaits your coming
> in the tent of meeting....
> So all beings that live by you
> praise your outpouring
> like a precious salve upon festering
> sores, upon fractured
> limbs. You convert them
> into priceless gems![20]

Building on the Trinitarian metaphor of the Holy Spirit as the bond of love between the Father and Son, Hildegard sings of the Spirit as the oneness within each person, in the communion of saints, and with God. Hildegard invites us to reflect on experiences of singing, in which our entire person is engaged—physical body, emotion, intellectual insight, desire. Music, like mystical experience, can sweep us up into the third heaven, taking us out of ourselves into an ecstatic state of personal, communal and cosmic harmony. In her theology, Hildegard names this power as a major work of the Spirit.

THE HOLY SPIRIT AND "GREENING"

One of the most well-known aspects of Hildegard's theology is her use of the term "greening" (*viriditas*). It is a pillar of her theology. She associates the Spirit with planting, watering, and blooming life. Spirit is linked with fruitfulness, vitality, physical and spiritual health, warmth, freshness, fertility, fecundity, and growth. *Viriditas* refers to the abundant, outpouring bounty of God, the fertility of nature, the aliveness of the soul—all signs of the presence of the Spirit. Commenting on the annunciation, Hildegard imagines Mary as the grass and the green earth; the Spirit is the dew that made her womb fruitful.[21]

In spiritual terms, Hildegard describes as "green" souls that are filled with virtue and fervor for God. They are alive in holiness. In contrast, she counsels clergy and nuns who are dry like a desert or tepid and weary of the spiritual journey (the Latin term is *taedium*, whence the English term "tedious") to renew their dedication and energy to follow the way of Christ. Most of us can point to times in our lives when we felt fully alive to God and other times when we felt a deadness or lethargy inside when it comes to being good and loving ourselves and others. Hildegard acknowledges that she had a tendency to depression, to see the dark side of things. But we also know that she had remarkable experiences of God's presence, which, in the end, won out. Her text reveals that she wanted to help, to teach others who were going through similar trials.

Along with being fully alive, nature is perhaps the most common way for people to notice God's presence. Each of the seasons of the year reminds us to reflect on the seasons of life and the cycle of death and rebirth. Hildegard wrote about Rupert, the patron of her monastery, as the "greenness of the finger of God" (*viriditas digiti Dei*). It is an apt and compelling metaphor, inviting all Christians to become "fingers" of God in the world—or "green thumbs"?—bringing genuine life and fecundity to everything and everyone we touch.

THE SPIRIT OF UNDERSTANDING

It is appropriate in a book on women's theology to call attention to the ways in which Hildegard understood the Spirit's contribution to understanding. Hildegard relied on reason and intellectual work to probe both the mysteries of nature (*scientia*) and the things of God (*theologia; sapientia*). In her book *Causes and Cures* she wrote:

> For if a person wishes to understand some work or art because
> of interest or desire, the Holy Spirit pours out its dew upon

this inclination, whence one learns and comprehends what he or she wishes to understand. Just as a father or mother answers a child when it tries to learn something from them, so also the Holy Spirit fosters human knowledge in any of the arts when the person seeks to learn it through inclination, desire, and diligence.[22]

In the process of "faith seeking understanding" the Holy Spirit is a partner in this search for knowledge. The Spirit's fiery presence enlightened Hildegard's mind, opening it to understand the meaning of the Scriptures and to write true doctrine in her heart and on paper. She describes the gentle, noninvasive nature of this presence:

> Inspiration from God was sprinkled into my soul's understanding like gentle drops of rain, just as the Holy Spirit filled Saint John the Evangelist when he suckled the profoundest revelation from the breast of Jesus, where his own understanding was touched by holy divinity so that he revealed hidden mysteries.[23]

While we correctly think of understanding and theology in terms of the Logos or second person of the Trinity, the Gospel of John extends this role to the Holy Spirit. John identifies the Spirit with truth—the Spirit teaches the truth (1 John 5:7–8). The Spirit not only teaches what Jesus taught, but most importantly, causes this teaching to take root in fertile hearts. Without the Holy Spirit, the Word of God remains distant and abstract. Without the Holy Spirit, we would not be able to hear the Word as a real, existential Word of life for us personally and for our world.

As a teacher, Hildegard had insight into the Spirit's pedagogical role. The "unlettered" Hildegard explained her understanding of the scriptures, of theology and doctrine, of medicine and music, through the unmediated tutoring of the Holy Spirit. In the *Scivias* she creates a poetic description of the Spirit's tutoring role in helping Christians absorb God's Word at a deep level. It is so important to her that she repeats this divine refrain throughout the text. "Therefore, whoever has knowledge in the Holy Spirit and wings of faith, let this one not ignore My admonition but taste it, embrace it and receive it in his soul."[24] This text mirrors what Hildegard experienced in the daily chanting of the psalms and the *lectio divina* she would have practiced as a Benedictine nun. The slow reading and repetition of sacred texts facilitates the Spirit's work of having the truth of the Word settle deep within.

Hildegard could have had no idea that one day she would take her place among the Doctors of the Church of whom she spoke: "And so the sense of the Scriptures that went forth from the mouth of the holy doctors broadened too; they searched the depths of the Scriptures' astringency and made it known to the many who learned from them, and thus they too enlarged their senses by knowing more of the wisdom and knowledge of the divine writings."[25]

Hildegard used the apostles at Pentecost as an example of this movement from unknowing to understanding. She wrote:

> And the Holy Spirit took their human fear from them.... And then they remembered with perfect understanding all the things they had heard and received from Christ with sluggish faith and comprehension.[26]

Hildegard must have had herself in mind here, but also those she judged to have strayed from the true teaching of the Church—both the heretical Cathars and the recalcitrant clergy within the Church. She wrote to persuade them to allow the true Word to take root and to return to lives of virtue and discipline. At times a kind of dualism emerges when Hildegard speaks of the flesh of Christ as a hindrance to the apostles' understanding of his message. She contrasts knowing Christ in the flesh with the purely spiritual knowledge that was given to the apostles by the Spirit at Pentecost.[27] Most theologies today give a prominent place not only to Christ's physical body but also to our own bodies as a way—along with the mind—to a deeper knowledge of God.

Hildegard's message about knowing in the Spirit invites us to reflect on how deeply we hear and appropriate the divine word. Does Pentecost happen in our lives so that, like Archimedes, we experience an "aha" experience of discovery and insight into the Word of God? Does the Spirit cause the "light to go on" so that we know the love of God and allow it to direct us in the concrete circumstances of everyday life? We may hear the Gospel every Sunday, or engage in prayer every day, but do these moments lead to new realizations of the existential meaning of the Good News that bear fruit in the world? There is a crucial difference between hearing the Gospel simply in our ears and hearing it in our very being. The latter leads inexorably to creative action for justice and a prophetic word of peace to power.

Such real, daily, concrete empowerment by the Sprit may be a struggle for those of us who are cultural Christians, that is, Christians who are born into Christian families, baptized as infants, and are perhaps even active within a Church. It is easy to think we understand God because we have been hearing about God for as long as we can remember. But Hildegard wants us to notice the difference between a more surface hearing and a deep listening that allows God to penetrate our inmost being. It is all too easy to think we are spiritual pilgrims, when, if we are honest, we may not even have gotten on the road yet.

Hildegard reminds us that the Spirit's power leads to ever more profound understandings of God and the world. Life becomes an ongoing conversion in which the Spirit penetrates more and more deeply over a lifetime. The Spirit leads us from glory to glory, to an ever deepening grasp of the things of God and the committed living out of this meaning of life. Hildegard also speaks to those who perceive the true meaning of the Word but do not have the courage to preach it. At the very outset of the *Scivias* she writes,

> And behold, He Who was enthroned upon that mountain cried out in a strong, loud voice saying, "O human, who are fragile dust of the earth and ashes of ashes! Cry out and speak of the origin of pure salvation, until those people are instructed,

who, though they see the inmost contents of the Scriptures, do not wish to tell them or preach them, because they are luke-warm and sluggish in serving God's justice. Unlock for them the enclosure of mysteries that they, timid as they are, conceal in a hidden and fruitless field. Burst forth into a fountain of abundance and overflow with mystical knowledge, until they who think you contemptible because of Eve's transgression are stirred up by the flood of your irrigation."[28]

HILDEGARD'S THEOLOGY TODAY

One of Hildegard's most valuable theological contributions is her ability to honor the tradition without sacrificing intellectual innovation and creativity. It is right to apply to Hildegard the line made famous by Frank Sinatra: "I did it my way." She knew and used the tradition—Origen, Gregory the Great, Ambrose, Augustine, and Jerome—but not in a slavish way. Her writing and her music reveal that she was always thinking, integrating the theological tradition with what she knew to be true in her experience and in response to what she perceived as the needs of her time. Peter Dronke says of Hildegard:

> Her approach to every problem—human, scientific, artistic, or theological—was her own. She took nothing ready-made. Her conviction that she saw the answers to the problems in her waking vision meant that she did not have to defer to estab-lished answers. Often we see she does not give a damn about these, however powerful their proponents. Many times she expresses herself courteously and modestly; yet when it comes to asserting what she believes to be right, she will do it bravely, outfacing all opposition.[29]

Hildegard stands as a model of a woman theologian who did not just accept the tradition as it was handed down to her. She absorbed this tradition and then transformed it into her own creative idiom. The result is an amazingly distinctive and fresh theology that is innovative but also traditional and even conservative on some points. This process needs to be carried on by all theologians today. And since women's voices in particular have not entered the theological picture until very recently, much work remains to be done.

Hildegard also challenges us to imagine a healthy, holy Church and to speak out against anything that threatens this holiness. Even though she received the official approbation of the Church to write and preach, she displayed notable courage in her harsh and honest criticism of ecclesial misconduct, greed, lust for power, and laxity. A prerequisite of this prophetic calling is to meditate on the Scriptures and the life of Jesus Christ and to interiorize the message in and through the power of the Spirit.

Hildegard loved the Church enough to want to reform it, to hope that it could be reformed, and to work for its renewal. The Church of the twenty-first century and the role of women within it are markedly different than in the twelfth. But Hildegard can inspire Christian women today to become theologians who reflect on the Good News in light of the signs of the times and to speak and act out of that reflection.

Finally, as a product of, and contributor to, her twelfth-century milieu, Hildegard reminds us of the connectedness of all things in God. We live in an age of academic, medical, and professional specialization. The sheer volume of knowledge makes it difficult even to entertain a picture of the whole. As a result, no one feels equipped to comment beyond their particular sphere of knowledge, and only a few engage in collaborative work that enables a vision of how things are connected. But we will not survive each in our own silo. Like Teilhard de Chardin, Hildegard saw the universe as one in God. In her sequence for the Holy Spirit, she wrote:

> O current of power permeating all
> in the heights upon the earth and
> in all the deeps:
> you bind together and gather
> all people together.[30]

God's unity radiates out to embrace the cosmos. Humans are unified in themselves as well as part of a greater unity of bodies, inanimate matter, plants, animals, and heavenly bodies. All are on the journey together. For Hildegard, the chapel, the garden, the infirmary, the court, and the family hearth are all the same room. Hildegard's theology confronts us, motivates us, encourages us to recognize the suffering earth and all its peoples and to work tirelessly in small and large ways to heal and care for it.

The ability and the will to imagine reality as one is more important than ever. Our experiences and knowledge of unity provide a foundation for imagining cosmic connectedness—nature, science, family, friendship, nation, Church, art, and music. Hildegard's integrated and coherent view of theology, cosmology, anthropology, and nature is remarkable. In addition, Hildegard's membership in a Benedictine community as leader and healer, and her work as composer and performer of drama, poetry, and music, provided her with concrete experience and insight into her oneness with God and the world. Singing must have been an activity in which Hildegard knew the flow of the Spirit's breath within her, the community, the Church, and the world. Hildegard knew the synergies and resonances between musical structures and the cosmic harmonies of the spheres.

THEOLOGICAL REFLECTION

- How does Hildegard inspire you to see yourself as a theologian?
- Do you think the Christian community should give more attention to the Holy Spirit than it currently does? Why or why not?
- How prominent is the Holy Spirit in your spiritual life? Identify one change that you might make to bring the Spirit to the forefront of your consciousness.
- Do you see yourself as a prophet in any way?
- Describe the role that music has in your life and spirituality. Do you ever link music with the Spirit?

CHAPTER THREE

Catherine of Siena (1347–1380)
Theology of Incarnation

W e move from Hildegard's twelfth-century Germany to Catherine of Siena's fourteenth-century Italy; from the monastic world of Benedictine nuns to the lay world of Dominican tertiaries; from the language of Latin to the vernacular, Italian; from a world of intellectual, political, and economic expansion to a world of decline, suffering and a mysticism of passionate intensity, exemplified in the *Cloud of Unknowing* and Julian of Norwich's *Shewings*. Unlike most women in Christian history, Catherine and Hildegard were both officially blessed by Rome as public authors, teachers, and preachers. In addition, Catherine was called upon to mediate conflicts in society and Church, and she had a very visible role as a papal counselor. Popes called upon her for advice, and she even addressed the curia in Rome during Urban VI's pontificate.

In the bestowal statement when she received the title, "Doctor of the Church" (1970), Paul VI praised Catherine for her gifts of exhortation and "wisdom in discourse."[1] The first quality points to her work in Church reform. The second points to her theology, a wisdom that weds knowledge to love. In the background of Catherine's theology is the female figure of Wisdom (*Hokmah* in Hebrew; *Sophia* in Greek—Proverbs 8 and 9; Wisdom 7), and the Wisdom/Sophia/Logos Incarnate of Matthew and John (Matthew 11:19; 12:42; 13:54; John 1).

LIFE AND WORKS

Catherine of Siena died on April 29, 1380, and her feast day is celebrated on this date each year. In her death as in her life, bodiliness played a prominent role. Most of her remains lie in the Roman Church of Santa Maria sopra Minerva under the main altar; her head rests in a reliquary in the Church of San Domenico in Siena—reminders of the medieval fascination with the power of holy bodies, seen as a mirror of the incarnate body of Christ. Like Francis of Assisi, her body was marked with Christ's wounds. During prayer in Pisa in 1375, her body assumed the form of Christ on the cross. She later reported that she had had a vision of Christ crucified during which Christ gave to her body the wounds on his body in a mystical and invisible manner.[2]

Pope Pius II, who came from an eminent Sienese family, canonized Catherine in 1461 and Pope Pius XII named her, with St. Francis of Assisi, copatron of Italy. In 1970, Paul VI declared Catherine of Siena a Doctor of the Church along with St. Teresa of Avila. In 1999, Pope John Paul II named her patron of Europe, along with Benedict of Nursia, Sts. Cyril and Methodius, Birgitta of Sweden, and Edith Stein.

Catherine's personality was large and complex. She inherited her fiery, determined qualities from her mother, Mona Lapa, who was described as talkative and volatile. Catherine's reflective, compassionate side is attributed to her father, Iacopo, who was of a calm and generous nature. In addition to the influence of her parents, Catherine may have absorbed the spirit of the self-confident, at times pompous, Sienese citizenry. Siena's dreams of grandeur are visible in the lofty architectural style of the city's main Campo, and the desire to be number one among neighboring Italian city-states, including Florence. Catherine's personality encompassed a lively social side, and a private, almost hermit-like dimension as well.

It all began in the large house on the Via dei Tintori ("the street of the tints"—her father was in the dyeing business), where Lapa gave birth to twenty-five children. Catherine was born on March 25, 1347, with her twin sister, Giovanna, who did not survive. They were the twenty-third and twenty-fourth children. Not long after their births, a last child was born, also named Giovanna, who died in 1363 at age fourteen. The names of ten of these children survive in the historical record.

Catherine's life was filled with life but also with many deaths. She was especially close to two members of her family: her older sister,

Bonaventura, who died in childbirth when Catherine was still young, and a cousin, Tommaso, who was absorbed into the Benincasa family when his parents died. He later became a Dominican priest and was one of Catherine's early confessors. Catherine would also have known the death associated with war and illness, especially the Black Plague.

Catherine reported having a vision of Christ at the very young age of six—childhood visions were also reported by other medieval women mystics. Accompanied by her brother Stefano on the way home from a visit with her sister Bonaventura, Catherine wrote about seeing an image of Christ in the sky over their local church, San Domenico. Dressed in white robes, holding a staff, and surrounded by a group of saints, Christ blessed her. This vision remained with her as a guide and guarantor of her later vocation to an active-contemplative life. After this experience, she became more introverted, more drawn to a life of solitude, penance, and prayer. This calling elicited significant conflict in her family, who had other plans for her, including a marriage that would enhance the family fortunes.

Catherine finally received permission to enter into solitude in a small room in her home in which she prayed, fasted, and did penance—sleeping on boards with a stone for a pillow. She took a private vow of virginity and had another mystical vision in which Christ invited her to be his bride.[3] While Catherine's preferred metaphors for perfect divine-human love were childhood and friendship, on occasion she spoke of herself as wedded to Christ—a common motif among several medieval mystics, celebrated in the Song of Songs. Catherine may also have known the story of St. Catherine of Alexandria, a patron of the Dominican Order and popular saint, who was said to have been taken up into heaven where she experienced a mystical marriage with Christ. Gradually, Catherine realized another aspect of her vocation: to follow in the steps of the apostles who served the Church and the world in public ministry.

Catherine's extreme fasting is the subject of much analysis and comment. Many holy ones—Clare of Assisi, Angela Foligno, and

Christina Markyate among them—were drawn to severe asceticism. Many, including Catherine, gradually concluded that such extreme practices were not truly holy, much less God's will—and later counseled followers on penitential moderation. Medieval knowledge of the body and the psyche, of course, did not include the insights of Freud and modern psychology. The term *anorexia* did not exist, but we can be certain that Catherine's eating habits led to malnutrition and the gradual impairment and cessation of her ability to ingest and digest food, bringing on an early death.

Eventually, Catherine followed her call to an active-contemplative life by joining a group of Third Order Dominican laywomen called the Mantellate. For the most part, they were mature women, often widows, so it took some maneuvering on the part of Mona Lapa to have the teenaged Catherine accepted into the group. The women were visible in the community as they trod the streets of Siena, serving the poor in their distinctive Dominican, black-and-white garb. As we will see, a major aspect of incarnational living is to be engaged in the real world of daily life, serving others in their material and physical needs. Catherine provides an exemplary model for this type of incarnational existence.

Gradually, Catherine's public persona grew. She became more involved in Italian politics, wider European conflicts, reform of corrupt clergy, and the difficulties of the papacy, including schism and multiple, concurrent popes. This involvement with the world also points to her incarnational theology. She lived, loved, argued with, and castigated a wide range of people. Some were her dearest friends; others were the object of her desire for their salvation and conversion from evil ways. Gathered around her was a large group of people she considered her family, with whom she travelled across Italy and France. She kept several scribes busy penning dictated letters—close women friends Cecca Gori and Lisa Colombini and later, a Sienese layman with literary talent, Neri di Landoccio Pagliaresi, and one of her favorite disciples, Stefano Maconi.

Perhaps it was inevitable that Catherine experienced a great deal of opposition, some of it hurtful and demeaning. Initially, she had to contend with her family who wanted her to marry and settle down. As Catherine's reputation grew, so did jealousy in the hearts of those who envied her popularity. Some of her sisters in the Mantellate and some friars in the local church attacked her reputation. At one point, she was banned from Mantellate meetings and even denied the sacraments. The distance of over six hundred years can blunt the pain, confusion, and anger these events must have caused Catherine.

One cleric criticized and castigated Catherine for her extreme fasts. She wrote back to him to say that no one more than she would like to be able to eat, but her early fasting had made her body incapable of normal intake of food. On occasion, Catherine was openly ridiculed in public, kicked and prodded during her spiritual trances by those who were convinced she was faking. At one point in Florence, an angry crowd pursued her through the streets, intending to kill her. Much to her disappointment, she was given refuge in the garden of a supporter and was denied her lifelong dream of martyrdom.

As an unlettered woman, Catherine was viewed with skepticism by the clergy and nobility alike. Her supporters attributed her biblical and theological insight to the Holy Spirit. Scholars acknowledge her intellectual acumen, her ability to shape her own theology from the scripture readings and preaching of the Mass and the Divine Office; listening to pious works read by others; counsel from personal confessors and advisors; and conversations with learned clerics such as her dear friend and confessor, Raymond of Capua, Giovanni Tantucci, Bartolomeo Dominici, and William Flete. But what is especially notable is what she did with this learning, weaving it into her experience of life, prayer, and ministry to establish her own unique, creative theology with its distinct flavor, emphases, and commitments.

In the midst of all this activity and conflict, Catherine managed to produce a serious body of theological work—a requirement for being named a Doctor of the Church.[4] Catherine's work was later often anthologized as she was the first woman to write and be published in an Italian dialect. Her corpus includes almost four hundred letters;

twenty-six prayers dictated while she was in ecstasy; and her major theological work, *The Dialogue,* written in 1377–1378. *The Dialogue* reveals how Catherine understood the mind and will of God, while the letters provide a glimpse into how her theology became visible in the concrete concerns of everyday life.

FOURTEENTH-CENTURY CONTEXT

Italian culture is known for its sensuousness. It is a culture that relishes and celebrates love, song, beauty, art, nature, and good food. Italy would be a good place to develop an incarnational spirituality grounded in sensual, material beauty. During Catherine's lifetime, there was growing interest in nature, literature, art, and the human person. Catherine shared the fourteenth-century stage with Dante (d. 1321), Chaucer (d. 1400), Birgitta of Sweden (d. 1373), Petrarch (d. 1374), and Boccaccio (d. 1375). Artists based their work on worldly observations that resulted in a greater naturalism and stronger emotional expression. Many scholars date the origins of the Renaissance and Italian humanism to the fourteenth century.

This materiality was also visible in Christianity. Churches, street shrines, religious paintings, and music told the stories of Christianity and inspired faith. Depictions of the events in Christ's life were visible on the walls of churches throughout the city. Siena was also famous for its devotion to the Virgin Mary, visible in frescoes, paintings, and altarpieces. Specific examples include Giotto's "Madonna Enthroned" which shows Mary in all her physical, bodily beauty, a queenly mother figure.[5] The luxuriousness of the adornment in the Siena Cathedral showcases the beauty and sacred nature of the material world, as well as the creativity of the human spirit.[6]

Faith was central to every aspect of life. Laymen belonged to religious confraternities linked to their professions—beer makers, blacksmiths, wheelwrights. These religious clubs provided solidarity, arranged religious celebrations and processions on major feast days, and performed charitable works for the poor. This might involve providing funds to families who could not afford a dowry or a proper burial for loved ones.

Catherine also lived in a plague-infested and war-torn century. Italian city-states fought with each other and with the papacy for land and power. A string of French popes abandoned Rome to reside in Avignon for a seventy-year exile. Civic and ecclesial politics were rife with corruption, scandal, and decadence. Shortly after Catherine's birth, major Italian banking institutions went bankrupt. In calamitous times, the poor suffer inordinately—often forced to live in hunger and poverty, taxed to pay for the follies of the elite. Thus, Catherine's theology had to deal with a strong sense of fear and insecurity. The urgency with which she approached everything was a response to the precarious state of Church and society.

Estimates suggest that perhaps sixty percent of the population in Siena and a third of Europe's urban population succumbed to the plague that visited Siena three times during Catherine's lifetime. In an outbreak in 1364, Catherine lost several sisters and nieces. Out of this chaos, there developed an atmosphere of penance throughout Europe. Pious practices, such as public penitential processions with participants flagellating themselves, surely influenced Catherine's piety. The theology of the time suggested that God was displeased with the human race, sending the plague as a warning to repent. We know Catherine was especially fond of Mary Magdalene, the repentant sinner.

Gradually, Catherine assumed the sins of the world, desiring to atone personally for the sins of other Christians. And yet her mature theology placed God's love, not God's wrath, at its center. For Catherine, the fact that human beings had been gifted with God's goodness and love made turning away from God all the more egregious. Her passion was for Christians to recognize that they were made in God's image—destined for the stars if only they would renounce selfishness and desire God in freedom and love.

In the political realm, the Middle Ages witnessed the emergence of nation states. We may wrongly presume that countries we call France, Italy, and England today always existed. But during the Middle Ages, such boundaries were not yet settled, and there were fierce battles among emperors, kings, popes, and nobles for land, power, and wealth. In addition to diplomacy and intrigue, a common means to attain these goals was war. The interminable conflict between France and England is known as the Hundred Years' War (1337–1453). War requires soldiers and a great deal of money, which meant taxes on those least able to pay. Since kings often identified their wars as "just," they felt free to tax churches as well, creating another level of animosity between civil and ecclesial bodies.

Catherine was directly involved in the struggles of the papacy. From 1309–1378, the Church experienced what is known as the Babylonian Captivity, a term coined by the Italian poet Petrarch to describe a period in which the popes resided in Avignon rather than Rome.

Reasons for this relocation included conflicts that made it dangerous for the pope to remain in Rome and pressure from the very powerful King Philip of France. Pope Clement V, previously the bishop of Bordeaux, was the first to reside in Avignon (1305–1314). In all, seven popes held residence there. Catherine was instrumental in convincing the last pope, Gregory XI (1370–1378) to return to Rome. If you visit the papal palace in Avignon, there is a small, colored, terra cotta bust of Catherine on the wall in one of the rooms. Gregory's successor, Urban VI, a rather unsavory character, called upon Catherine for counsel during his stormy reign. A tranquil time in the Church this was not.

The chaos and violence of the period affected the pastoral and theological responses that might have been quite different in an era of peace and integrity. How did people interpret the discord and violence in Church and society? What role did they see God playing in their lives? Catherine spoke of the "darkness that has come over holy Church!" and felt "surrounded by many enemies."[7] These "signs of the times" during Catherine's lifetime make up the context for understanding her theological ideas and pastoral responses. They also provide insight into the intensity of her prayer and action, and explain why the Church sought insight and support from a well-known, holy, Italian woman. Calamitous times call for strong remedies.

We turn now to Catherine's theology of incarnation, finding clues in her letters, prayers, and in her major theological work, *The Dialogue.*[8]

Themes include Catherine's use of everyday language and metaphor to express theological ideas; the call to intimate union between Christ and human beings; a lay lifestyle in the Church; a refusal to limit the holy to monastic enclosure; metaphors of clothing, hunger, blood and the bridge.

CATHERINE'S THEOLOGY OF INCARNATION

Catherine has the distinction of being the first Italian woman published in the vernacular—her local Tuscan dialect. The vocabulary and metaphors used to express her theology are taken from daily life. Bernard McGinn compiles a long list of examples: anvil, bed, book, bridge, cell, city, ship, fishhook, house, key, knights, mirror, trees.[9] Catherine expresses incarnational theological meaning through metaphors for clothing, eating, drinking, hunger, and thirst. A striking example of her use of physical imagery can be found in her description of her marriage to Christ. Catherine does not receive a ring, but a very physical object— Christ's foreskin, traditionally removed at circumcision. It is hard to think of a more graphic example of the use of physical imagery.

Like many of her contemporaries, Catherine was drawn to the human Christ as tender lover and spouse, as generous giver, whose selfless love for the world led to his suffering and death on the cross. Catherine brings these everyday images to life, leading the reader from the language of the text to the immediacy of their physical reality.

Of the New Testament authors, Catherine favored Paul and John— texts heard at Mass and the Divine Office that she would have memorized, making them integral to her thought patterns and linguistic expression. She may have identified with Paul who, like Catherine, was taken up into the third heaven of visions and rapture (2 Corinthians 12:4). Catherine also had to defend her ministry and preaching against detractors. But she was no doubt also drawn to Paul's powerful Christology and the intimacy of the divine-human relationship. Paul's exhortation to live "in Christ crucified" (1 Corinthians 1:22– 24) grounds Catherine's conviction that Christ "makes of her another himself."[10] Catherine's theological wisdom reflects Paul's words about the Spirit's gift of wisdom (1 Corinthians 12:8); and his belief that wisdom should benefit the entire community (1 Corinthians 13). In his *Life of Catherine,* Raymond of Capua acknowledged the effectiveness of Catherine's preaching when he writes of God's promise to her: "I will give you a mouth and a wisdom which none shall be able to resist."[11]

Catherine's lifestyle reveals an incarnational perspective. Her eventual choice to become a Mantellata—a lay member of the Dominican Third Order—reveals her desire and her openness to God's call to live a life of active engagement in the world. Women who were financially able sought religious life in an enclosed monastery, shut off from the world. In contrast, Catherine lived a synthesis of the mystical way and public activity. Thus, it is legitimate to speak of her theology as a practical theology. The third orders of the Dominicans and Franciscans allowed for a mixed life for women as well as men—a life that embraced social and civic engagement as well as serious prayer.

An example that shows Catherine's positive attitude toward action can be found in late 1378 when she was asked to convene a council of elders to help Pope Urban VI deal with corruption and hostile enemies. She invited William Flete to join this council—an Englishman who had given up an academic life to become a hermit in the woods at Lecceto in Tuscany. He and Catherine were lifelong friends, and she valued his wisdom and holiness. When he declined her invitation, she wrote to his secretary, Brother Antonio, with some pique: "It's my experience that for God's true servants every place is their place and every time is their time. When it's time to abandon their own consolation and embrace difficulties for God's honor, they do it. And when it's time to leave the woods and go to public places because God's honor demands it, they go."[12] She argued that God does not privilege certain places as holy, to the exclusion of other locales. She warns Flete not to be so attached to the tranquility of his familiar and comfortable retreat in the woods.

In this letter to Flete, Catherine tells us two things about her incarnational theology. First, she denies that there are some places and times that, by their very nature, are more godly than others. It is appropriate to extend this embrace of action beyond church and religious life to all sectors of society. Catherine would support a vocation to be a sacrament of God's presence in the factory, the office, the bank, the home, the hospital, the assembly line.

Second, she reminds us that when the Church and the world are in need, we are not to cling to familiar comforts but rather venture into difficulty and danger. In Catherine's time (and in certain places today), that danger could involve losing one's life. God's desire for our good is not fulfilled in isolation, but through the concrete, loving activity of embodied persons in history. Her theology offers clues as to how believers can better integrate their faith with work, marriage and family, relationships, politics, and economics.

On the other hand, the medieval Church lived in a carefully calibrated hierarchical universe. The idea of hierarchy was inherited from Pseudo-Dionysius, a fifth-century Syrian cleric. In his works *The Celestial Hierarchy* and *The Ecclesiastical Hierarchy,* he envisions the Church as a reflection of heaven with its hierarchies of angels. This idea was translated into a vigorous debate about whether diocesan clergy, enclosed contemplatives, or mendicant monks held the highest place in the Church. Laity were not part of this discussion, as they were consistently placed at the bottom of the ladder of holiness.

It is unfortunate but not surprising then, that Catherine embraced this cultural worldview. It is visible in her letters to monastic communities where she encouraged reform, using the idea of monastic superiority to goad her readers to live better lives. She compared vowed religious to angels. She wrote: "Since God has made you worthy of being in the angelic state, don't choose to put yourself in the human state. It is layfolk who are in the human state. They are called to the common state, but you are in the state of perfection."[13]

But in other settings, Catherine emphasizes the importance of baptism, which includes all members of the Church. God tells Catherine that God has made allowances for those who remain in the world—the wealthy, the powerful, the married—so long as they reject "the venomous sting of selfish sensuality."[14] Everything is good because it has been created by God and is to be used "with a good and holy will" in the service of life not death.[15] In a letter to women monastics in Bologna, Catherine emphasized how Christ's blood gives baptism its redemptive power. She wrote: "Everyone, no matter what his or her state in life, must do this for God who is a respecter not of states of life but of holy desires."[16]

Catherine was also a woman of her time inasmuch as she linked sin with the physical body. She wrote of her body as wretched, as that part of herself from which she wished to be freed in death. She described it "as a perverse law that is always fighting against the spirit."[17] Throughout much of Christian history, Paul's Letter to the Romans, where he distinguishes between the inner, spiritual self that is in harmony with the law of God and the external body that is a war with this law (Romans 7:22–23), has been given a dualistic interpretation. Paul uses the term *body* to point not to human physical flesh but to sin, to anything that moves us away from God, and *spirit* as anything that moves us toward God.

On the other hand, Catherine's theology is replete with talk of material reality, bodily functions, and everyday life. As the daughter of a dyer, Catherine was familiar with various types of material and often used the metaphor of clothing to describe the spiritual life. This knowledge draws her to use Paul's idea of being clothed with Christ crucified.[18] She entreated her friends and followers to clothe themselves in virtue and especially in "Christ gentle Jesus." Since clothing is the substance closest to the flesh of our bodies, Catherine suggests an intimate relationship between our humanity and Christ's. As a woman, Catherine's awareness of her body and the materiality of the world provided a provocative theological link to Christ's humanity.

Nourishment is another important theological metaphor for Catherine. She understood that she could not nourish others without being nourished herself at the breasts of divine charity. While Catherine never bore or nursed children, she provides a vivid description of this intimate encounter. Like the child who "takes the breast of its mother, applies its mouth, and by means of the flesh it draws milk…we must attach ourselves to that breast of Christ crucified."[19] It is Christ's humanity that suffered pain and we cannot be nourished without sharing in that pain. Catherine extends the metaphor of nourishment to themes of spiritual hunger for God and others. One of her favorite descriptions for loving the neighbor was "eating souls on the table of the cross." In all these senses, Catherine's theology is infused with an incarnational perspective.

For Catherine, Christ's humanness is the linchpin of redemption and of the entire Christian life. In a letter from Rome to her followers in Siena, Catherine summarized her Christology in which Christ's humanity is the anchor. I cite this passage at length since meditation on such a passage brings one into the heart of Catherine's theology.

> His [Christ's] humanity was a wall that held within itself the fire of the eternal Godhead which was joined with that same humanity. And the fire of divine charity spilled out through the opened-up wall, Christ crucified. His precious wounds poured out blood mixed with fire, because it was by the fire of love that his blood was shed. From this fountain we draw the water of grace, since it was not merely through his humanity but by the power of the Godhead that human sin was washed away and we were restored to grace.[20]

Catherine combines a range of images and metaphors to communicate the power and effectiveness of God's choice to enter history as a human being and to open the door to the freedom and holiness of the entire human race through the cross.

Since theology grows out of concrete life experience, different lives produce different "flavors" of theology—male/female; rich/poor; celibate/married; city/country. Catherine's ability to use familiar daily experiences to express profound theological truths continues to enrich the spiritualities of those who read her work. Catherine and many of her sister mystics identified closely with the humanity of Christ. They "became the flesh of Christ, because their flesh could do what his could do: bleed, feed, die and give life to others."[21]

Bernard McGinn describes Catherine's theology as "the least apophatic" of mystical theologies.[22] Catherine's texts announce that "God is...HERE, addressing Catherine, and through Catherine, the world."[23] Surrounded by corruption, and what must have seemed like the absence of the divine in Church and society, Catherine was driven to reinvest the world with God's presence. Her theology is incarnational in its political as well as its mystical aspects. She responded to a call that placed her in the midst of the problems of the world and Church. In symbolic and real terms, this meant reform at every level, returning the papacy to Rome, and the Holy Land to Christianity. Catherine even agreed to support a crusade to the Holy Land, though it never got off the ground.

Two of Catherine's main Christological metaphors serve as examples of her incarnational theology: the blood and the bridge.

THE BLOOD

Her favorite images of blood and bridge serve as examples of how Catherine's theology is oriented toward incarnation. The image of blood is a leitmotif that runs throughout her writings (there are almost two thousand references). Blood captures the idea at the heart of Catherine's theology—God's incredible, amazing love for humanity and the world is expressed most powerfully in Jesus Christ on the cross. The image of blood becomes a mantra in her letters, most of which begin: "I Caterina, slave of the servants of Jesus Christ, am writing to you in his precious blood."

The theme of blood is found in many world mythologies as a symbol of love and life. In the New Testament, Paul and John emphasize blood in the context of the cross, the Eucharist, and cleansing from sin. Bernard McGinn writes: "Blood is life, blood is food and drink, blood is bath, blood is bond and mortar, blood is ransom, blood is key, blood is door, blood is clothing, blood is reproach, blood is witness, blood is even grace, and more."[24] In one letter, Catherine wishes that she could sweat blood that would heal the world's sin.[25]

As we have seen, Catherine lived in a time literally filled with the blood of war and illness. In her relationship with Christ, she enters into, and drinks from, the wound in his side; she exchanges the wound of love. In the power of the blood, sin is wiped away. Catherine believed that only Christ's blood could satisfy the thirst of humanity. The blood spilled at Christ's circumcision was not enough, requiring the additional blood spilled when the lance opened his heart on the cross. When we drink this blood, we become like drunken people—the more we drink, the more we want to drink; in love, pain becomes refreshment. In declaring Catherine a Doctor of the Church, Paul VI links drinking and divine truth, speaking of Catherine's "lucid, profound and inebriating absorption of divine truths."[26] Catherine's theology is born not only of the mind, but also of the heart and spirit. It is an affective theology, the fruit of both her intelligence and her love affair with God.

Blood also symbolizes the fountain of compassion for all Christians. The fruit of Christ's blood is love of neighbor. Catherine unites drinking from the heart of the crucified with drinking from the wounds of our neighbors. Many are familiar with the story of Catherine's care of Andrea, a very difficult patient suffering from cancer. At one point, Catherine drinks the water in which she had just bathed Andrea's tumorous breasts. She wrote to a senator from Siena, "The more you love God, the more your love will reach out to your neighbors, helping them spiritually and materially as you have the opportunity and time to serve them."[27] Catherine also reminds her readers that there is no blood without fire, suggesting that she sees the Spirit as a full, equal participant in the work of salvation.[28] Along with Christ, the Holy Spirit is like a wet nurse at whose breasts we can be nourished—enabling loving care of those in need.

THE BRIDGE

Catherine also sees Christ's life/body as a bridge, dedicating an entire section in *The Dialogue* to this theme.[29] She uses her incarnational eye to enflesh the statement in John: "I am the Way, the Truth and the Life"

(14:16). Catherine sees Christ in his life and in his very body as a bridge. Bernard of Clairvaux is in the background here. He interpreted the kiss of the Song of Songs as an ascension to union with God in three stages (feet, breasts, lips). Catherine imagines three steps across the body of Christ. Bernard also wrote: "Only by means of the body do we gain those merits that lead to a life of blessedness. St. Paul sensed this, saying: 'The invisible things of God are understood through the things he has made' (Romans 1:20)."[30]

The Christian becomes a true image of God by walking from Christ's feet to his side/heart, to his mouth. Below the bridge is sin, a dangerous, raging river that separates us from God. The bridge of Christ's crucified body is the gift and sign of God's goodness, allowing sinful humanity to walk on the "feet of their affection" to reconnect with God.[31] When the faithful hear the voice of Christ calling them, they do not simply walk, but run over the bridge, anxious to learn the doctrine that is written on the very body of Christ crucified.[32] In his free choice to become human and die out of love for us, Christ becomes this bridge. The way across requires imitation of Christ's virtues—the shops on the bridge provide food, respite, and community.

The Human Person

Catherine's incarnational theology also includes an exalted yet realistic concept of the human person. She commends the Trinity for being willing to share with humans "all that you are, high eternal Trinity!" Catherine answers her own question when she asks God why God created humanity with such dignity. "With unimaginable love you looked upon your creatures within your very self, and you fell in love with us."[33] This divine reflection confers great dignity on the human race, along with high expectations of the virtues required to live up to this divine image (Genesis 1:27).

In an intriguing passage echoing Hildegard of Bingen, Catherine imagines the human person as a complex system of harmonious sounds in which the great chords of the soul's powers—free will and intellect—are blended with the small chords of the body's senses and organs, creating a rousing sound of life (as opposed to the dead sound of sinners). Every instrument plays in good holy actions, creating a hook by which sinners are caught and converted from death to life.[34]

We hear Augustine in Catherine's portrait of the human person. It is a passage worthy of extended reflection. God says to Catherine:

> I made the soul after my own image and likeness, giving her memory, understanding, and will. The understanding is the most noble aspect of the soul. It is moved by affection, and it in turn nourishes affection. Affection is love's hand, and this hand fills the memory with thought of me and of the blessings I have given. Such remembrance makes the soul caring instead of indifferent, grateful instead of thankless. So each power lends a hand to the other, thus nourishing the soul in the life of grace.
>
> The soul cannot live without love. She is always trying to love something because love is the stuff she is made of, and through love I created her. This is why I said that it is affection that moves the understanding, saying, as it were, "I want to love, because the food I feed on is love." And the understanding, feeling itself awakened by affection, gets up, as it were, and says, "If you want to love, I will give you something good that you can love." And at once it is aroused by the consideration of the soul's dignity and the indignity into which she has fallen through her own fault.[35]

This holistic portrait of the human person emphasizes the harmony of the various dimensions of human life and the prominent role given to feeling as well as to understanding.

But there is no doubt that Catherine has a stark sense of sin. It seems outrageous to her that humans would turn against this generous, gift-giving God. For Catherine, the soul, by nature, always desires what is good, but selfish love clouds the ability to judge rightly. We get things backward; we become confused, even frenzied, rushing about, grabbing onto things that, in the end, are fleeting and destructive. In a letter to her friends in Florence, Bartol Usimbardi, his wife, Orsa, and a tailor, Francesco di Pipino, and his wife, Catherine writes that since we have been released from slavery by the cross, "it is completely our own fault if we don't walk along that way."[36]

Catherine underlines the inviolability of human freedom, a creative counterpoint to God's providence. God says to her: "I created you without your help, but I will not save you without your help."[37] For Catherine, God may test humanity, provoke growth with suffering, and even permit the devil to tempt souls. But God never violates or coerces human free will—an arena that is off-limits to the devil as well.[38] Participation in the incarnation is not automatic but depends on our desires. Catherine warns against purely external and superficial engagement with God. She encourages her followers to attend to their deepest desires because it is precisely these authentic desires within their hearts that make possible the link between the human and the divine.

In addition to her acute sense of sin, Catherine has the experience of being nothing in the face of the awesome love and perfection of God. God says to her: "You are she who is not, and I am he who is." Catherine is not engaging in false humility, but simply speaking the truth. When Catherine understood who God is; when she allowed God's enormous love to penetrate her being, she discovered that she did not look like much. This experience led her to a profound and spontaneous sense of humility. Her language is extreme. But when she speaks of herself as a base lie, as an agent of non-being, she is talking about a self that has lost track of the truth that her being depends entirely on having been created by God. Over and over again, she hammers home the point that this sorry state has been transformed by the incarnation. Our "true" self reflects God, participates in God. We are called by the divine Spouse to intimate love. This amazing gift is offered by God to all, freely and generously. It is pure gift.

Catherine calls us to be on the lookout for this God. Each person will discover this God in a unique way—an experience of beauty, love, forgiveness, generous sacrifice—the smile of a child, the first glimpse of the Grand Canyon, a donated organ, betrayal, persecution. In such circumstances, we stand in awe and feel infinitesimally small and unworthy. Life then truly becomes gift. Such experiences give access to Catherine's theology. For her, God is great not simply because of God's unimaginable goodness, but because God has chosen in love to share that goodness with creation and the human race. God pours out Godself in creation, incarnation, and Eucharist. God gifts us with every breath in every fiber of our being. Catherine prays:

> O fire of love!
> Was it not enough to gift us
> with creation in your image and likeness,
> and to create us anew to grace in your Son's blood,
> without giving us yourself as food,
> the whole of divine being,
> the whole of God?
> What drove you?
> nothing but your charity,
> mad with love as you are![39]

Catherine's God is awesome and amazing because of love. The existential aspect of her theology involves her faithful trust that God in Christ has loved from all eternity and will never stop loving the world.

SELF-KNOWLEDGE

Catherine speaks of the mirror image of the divine and the human in terms of the intimate relationship between self-knowledge and knowledge of God. The origin of this idea goes back to Catherine's childhood. When her family imposed on her the role of servant, she devised the practice of going within herself to satisfy her hunger for inner prayer. She called it her "cell" or her "house." Later, this cell was transformed from a place of escape to a place with windows for love and a door for voicing her theology. It is in this sacred interior place that we learn the truth of God's goodness and image within us.[40]

It is instructive to reflect on the contrasts between self-knowledge as Catherine used the term, and our post-Freudian description of the self in terms of ego, superego, and id. For Catherine, authentic self-knowledge is a profoundly *theological* truth since knowledge of self and knowledge of God mirror each other. Self-knowledge means knowing the following truths: we are created in God's image; we are the recipients of God's infinite goodness; we are sinners; we are loved by God in indescribable ways; and we are freed from sin in the cross, invited to share the very life of God.

Catherine describes the closeness of God as unimaginable intimacy, an intimacy arranged by God: "And so that you might have no excuse for looking at my affection, I found a way to unite gift and giver: I joined the divine nature with the human…. You cannot look at my gift without looking at me, the Giver."[41] God's Word is "engrafted in our humanity."[42] God is in us and we are in God like the "fish is in the sea and the sea is in the fish."[43] Catherine loved to repeat that God is madly in love, even drunk, with love for creation.[44] She addresses God: "O mad lover! It was not enough for you to take on our humanity: you had to die as well!"[45] Her language about the intimate closeness of God is as extreme as that about God's awesome otherness. Her relationship with God imparts a joy that causes the parts of her body to melt and "disintegrate like wax in the fire."

THE TRINITY

Catherine's theology of incarnation is also a theology of the Trinity. The God who desires to embrace humanity intimately is the entire Trinity.[46] Catherine uses the homey metaphor of baking to portray the oneness of divine power, wisdom and fire: "The person of the incarnate Word was penetrated and kneaded into one dough with the light of my Godhead, the divine nature, and with the heat and fire of the Holy Spirit, and by this means you have come to receive the light."[47] The Trinity encounters the world and each of us as a community of love.

Contemporary theology has much to say about the intimate communion within the Trinity.[48] The Greek word is *perichoresis*, a term that describes the dynamic, loving interpenetration of each person within the other. Each person of the Trinity draws identity and life from the other persons. Picasso's painting, *La Ronde de la Jeunesse* ("The Dance of Youth") captures this idea. The painting portrays a circle of dancing figures holding on to each other in the power of the movement, like an eternal, joyful dance.[49] If we combine this modern, dynamic image with Catherine's theology of the Trinity, we find ourselves both blessed and challenged. We discover that God is the epitome of everything we cherish about communal love; and that every Christian is invited in Baptism to join this divine communal dance.

In Catherine's anthropology, human persons, like the divine persons, are embedded in community. In *The Dialogue* she shows how virtue and vice are always played out in the ebb and flow of human relationships.[50] Her sense of community extends to the entire communion of saints—the apostles, prophets, and martyrs who have gone before as well as the faithful and leaders in the Church. While she herself functioned as a leader—a woman who stepped outside the accepted norms of female behavior—she was also profoundly conscious that we are interdependent beings who must rely on each other and God for our very existence and well-being.[51]

CATHERINE'S THEOLOGY TODAY

Catherine's theology was forged in the midst of enormous cultural and spiritual disruption and suffering. She wrote her theology from the trenches, etching it in deeply incarnational patterns. Her use of accessible, everyday imagery allows us to enter into her thought. Her theology invites us to reflect on our own theological images. Her ideas about God and the human person are inseparable. Catherine challenges us to recognize the divine goodness within us—to be in awe of it and to live up to its calling. Her most enduring theological message is this:

the incarnation provides the power for us to know that we are made "in Christ." Our human destiny is to live out in concrete, historical time and place, the gift of divine goodness in us.

Incarnational theology is characterized by a sacramental consciousness that views every aspect of the universe as irreversibly holy—in spite of our attempts to destroy it through sin. Incarnation is a deepening of the truths of creation, grace, and Holy Spirit, reminding us of the profound integration of Christian doctrines. It rejects dualistic outlooks that pit matter against spirit: the sensual against the cerebral, emotion against mind, leisure against work, women against men.

Incarnational theology takes seriously the effects of Christ's taking on human flesh. From this perspective, it no longer makes sense to distinguish the "sacred" (good, religious) and the "secular" (bad, profane). It rightly names the enemy as "sin," not "the world" (i.e., nature politics, education, corporations, film, sex, money, etc.), which is intrinsically holy because of Christ's entering history and becoming fully human. Nothing, in and of itself, is prevented from sharing in the divine life. Thus, the call to become saints and theologians is worked out primarily in the midst of everyday life—love, joy, sorrow, struggle, work, nature, relationships, ecosystems, violence, illness, suffering, and death.

Incarnational theologies can move us to attend to the world with a long, loving, compassionate gaze that leads to active, passionate care. We nurture a love that finds concrete, earthly solutions when we are attuned to the utter sacredness of it all.

For Catherine, the work of the Christian life is to live "in the blood," that is, in service to others. Since we cannot love God as God deserves, love of neighbor becomes the centerpiece of the virtuous life. Later, in sixteenth century Spain, Teresa of Avila will echo Catherine's voice that the only way to love God is through love of neighbor. Genuine faith is active in the world and therefore complex and difficult. Just as knowledge of self and knowledge of God can never be separated, so love of God and love of neighbor function as two sides of the same coin (Matthew 22:37–40). None of this is possible without the incarnation and Catherine's relentless spotlight on the cross.

Catherine learned the hard way to see her own physical body as holy. In this, she was certainly a woman of her time. Like Francis of Assisi, her fierce desire to suffer with and for Christ led her to an ascetic life that ruined her body. But her faithful attention to life in the Spirit led to change.

Catherine wrote to Monna Agnesa, a Mantellata, about the dangers and illusions of making penance the foundation of the spiritual life. Catherine criticizes those who attend more to killing their bodies than to killing off selfish will.[52] And a few months before her death, she wrote to her dearest friend, Raymond of Capua, who had just become a Dominican provincial, "And as much as you can in your position, be devoted to your physical as well as your spiritual cell."[53] This openness to change her mind is in itself a helpful spiritual model.

There are commonalities between the Church of Catherine's time and that of our own. The particular failings of the Church are different, but equally serious. We do not worry about having two, or even three, duly elected, competing pontiffs. We do not have large numbers of clergy with clandestine wives and bastard children. Church leaders no longer openly buy and sell Church offices or pass them down to sons, cousins, or nephews. Bishops no longer have their own armies, and they rarely live outside their dioceses.

But we struggle with clericalism; the pedophilia scandal; the unwillingness to be held accountable; the refusal to engage in honest, open conversation about pressing issues in the Church and in the world. And while Catherine, the female, held a prominent, public role in Church affairs, she was an exception. Knowing her story compels us to persevere in asking the question about women's roles in the Church. In spite of its failings, Catherine understood the Church as the font of grace, the body of Christ, the vine of true life, possessing the light of Christ. To be cut off from the institution—no matter how corrupt—meant to be cut off from the humanity of Christ, which meant to be cut off from the flow of grace. Pope Francis's leadership reflects some of Catherine's openness and honesty—offering hope to all.

Catherine's theological legacy invites women especially, to reflect on their experience as a source for their theologies. Her recourse to metaphors of eating, drinking, feeding, nursing, engagement, and marriage reminds us of the sacralizing effect of incarnation on all creation. Today we would add metaphors of the corporate world, manual labor, athletics, entertainment, art, medicine, scholarship, and much more. Her public persona and political engagement challenge the limits we set on the fruit of Incarnation. Medieval scholar Caroline Walker Bynum notes that many medieval women "reached God not by reversing what they were [women] but by sinking more fully into it."[54]

A compelling source and fruit of Catherine's theology is her courage. Her passionate relationship with the crucified and risen Christ bore fruit in a fearlessness grounded in love. Her theology is like a reverse image of Thérèse of Lisieux's Little Way, although both witnessed to amazing courage. Catherine was impatient with the faint of heart—those who preferred to remain with the familiar and the comfortable—especially when they were called to help a floundering Church and suffering world. Her prophetic voice called attention to the sins of the Church, including the highest ranks of the clergy. She does not mince words. She described the Church as having a dirty face, being impure and selfish with bloated pride, avarice, and wretched, abominable self-centeredness. Selfish clergy are like flies who taste the sweetness of Christ's blood but abandon the altar, the sacraments and the administration of the Church. God speaks: "Not only does such iniquity stink to me, but even the devils find this wretched sin repugnant."[55]

Slander, ridicule, even violence do not deter her. She wrote to Raymond of Capua: "I long to see you courageous, not afraid of anyone at all."[56] Fear is a killer of life and love. In the depths of her thought, Catherine reveals how intense, committed love banishes fear and undue concern for self. To Brother Tommaso, she warns against having a cold heart. She wrote: "I long to see you dying of passion" whose source "is the soul's fervent desire for God. Up then dearest son! Let's be responsive to the great need we see in holy Church! Roar your desire over these dead, and let's not rest until God turns the eye of his mercy [on them]."[57] In all things, Christ is the model and the means that make such a life possible.

Catherine's identification with Christ emboldened her to assume, with Christ, the call of redeeming love, and she invited others to continue this divine mission. She wrote to Raymond of Capua: "Conceive, my children, and give birth to this child, the human race, with hatred and sorrow for sin and with blazing and yearning love."[58] Her vision was universal. Incarnation and creation go hand in hand. Since God created the whole world, it was held in God's hands, and everyone and everything belonged to God.

The beauty of Catherine's courage is enhanced by her awareness and acceptance of her nothingness before the face of God. She repeatedly calls attention to her non-being when she gazes at the fullness of divine being. Suzanne Noffke has come to believe that Catherine's deepest legacy is "the paradox of her greatest weakness."[59] The apostle Peter was a model for her. She attributes his strength to his ability to "let go of himself" and "seek nothing but Christ crucified."[60]

Catherine's incarnational theology is more than a theory. It is an existential, on-the-ground, living theology that involves real people, suffering, joy, and failure. She lived her life honestly, refusing to excuse herself from the path she encouraged others to live. She entreated her disciples not to judge the intentions of others, and yet in her fight for the Church of her vision, she spoke a prophetic word against corrupt behaviors. Few saints wrote of their sinfulness in such stark terms. But her loving openness to God meant that she also grew in holiness and grace. Catherine embraced redemption in her own brokenness when, at her death, her certainty gave way. But she embraced the truth of God's message to her and she knew the truth of God's message to her: "Do you know, daughter, who you are and who I am? If so, you have blessedness in your grasp. You are the one who is not, and I am the one who is."[61]

Theological Reflection

- For you, what is the most important aspect of Catherine's theology of incarnation? Why? How might this part of her theology help those wishing to live the Christian life today?

- Which of Catherine's images caught your imagination—blood, bridge, the human person, self-knowledge, or the Trinity? Why?

- When you hear the term *self-knowledge* what comes to mind? Is it a primary way for you to discover and encounter Christ? What means do you use to attain self-knowledge? What is one of the most precious things you know about yourself? Does this trait influence your Christology?

- Catherine's theology was born in the midst of opposition. Reflect on your experience of struggle. For what do you stand up and why? Do you stick to your guns when others criticize or move away from you? How do you relate this to Christ crucified?

- Pray Psalm 115, repeating the antiphon "Not to us, O Lord, but to your name give glory" to catch the spirit of Catherine's theology and spiritual way.

CHAPTER FOUR

Teresa of Avila (1515–1582)
Theology of the Human Person

In 1614, in Madrid, Spain, fireworks exploded to celebrate the beat-ification of Teresa of Avila. Even the king attended the Mass in her honor. The image of Teresa displayed at this event portrayed her holding a palm leaf in one hand (virginity) and a golden pen in the other (eloquence).[1] Only thirty-five years earlier, she had been under scrutiny by the Inquisition. The papal nuncio had called her "a rest-less gadabout, a disobedient and contumacious woman who invented wicked doctrines…and taught others, against the commands of St. Paul, who had forbidden women to teach."[2] In between, in 1588, only six years after Teresa's death, Fray Luis de Léon had her works published, an event that would seem to confirm the legitimacy of her writing.

But the following year the Inquisition inaugurated a campaign to have her works banned. Challenging male privilege was unacceptable, as was the very idea that learned men would take instruction from a woman or publicly acclaim her as a teacher of prayer or doctrine. How quickly things change. Some four hundred years later, on September 27, 1970, Paul VI declared Teresa of Avila a Doctor of the Church, noting the extraordinary action of the Holy Spirit in her teaching on the inner dynamics of prayer. Naming the first female Doctor of the Church was an astonishing departure from tradition. He defended this choice of a non-ordained woman by noting that Teresa exercised the priesthood of all the faithful bestowed in the waters of baptism.[3]

Life and Works

Violent, bloody events that took place in the decades prior to Teresa's birth would have serious repercussions for her. These included the marriage and rule of Ferdinand and Isabella in 1469, which brought a vision of a united Spain based on ethnic and religious purity of blood. By 1492, refusal to convert to Christianity meant expulsion for Muslims and Jews. For the previous eight hundred years, Christians, Jews, and Muslims had lived on the same land in a multicultural mix that could be, in turn, peaceful or acrimonious. Internal and external threats to these communities created shifting alliances—each group turning to whatever group might come to their aid in the moment. And yet these diverse cultural gifts of art, architecture, language, literature, music, and religion brought Spanish civilization to new heights.

It was in this context that Teresa de Cepeda y Ahumada was born on March 28, 1515, in Avila, Spain, to Doña Beatriz who came from a noble family, and Don Alonso Sanchez de Cepeda, a successful merchant.[4] Don Alonso had two children from his first marriage. Alonso and Beatriz had a large, loving, prosperous, well-respected family with ten children. Teresa would have been taught to read and write, and she was influenced by her mother's fondness for popular novels recounting the exploits of knights and their ladies. Her father had an extensive library of classic texts that included many theological and spiritual books. In November of 1528, when Teresa was thirteen, her mother died.

It took until the 1940s for researchers to discover that Teresa came from Jewish ancestry. Her paternal grandfather, Juan Sánchez, was a Jew forced to convert to Christianity. In 1485 he was accused of back-sliding and was subjected to a humiliating punishment in which Jews who continued to practice Judaism secretly were paraded through the streets of Toledo wearing yellow tunics called *sambenitos*. Arriving at the local church, these garments, with their family names emblazoned on them, were hung on the walls of the Church as a permanent reminder of their laxness. Understandably, this personal family history would deeply affect the way Teresa understood social relationships and the value and role of the human person.

To put this conflict behind them, Teresa's family moved to Avila where they once again became financially successful. The growing para-noia about "pure blood" led to a practice whereby "new Christians" with financial means could purchase certificates that testified (falsely) to the purity of their history as pure-blooded "old Christians." This opened social and professional doors that were otherwise off-limits to new Christians. And yet, converted Jews and Muslims were always suspected of infidelity to the Christian faith and remained outsiders. They were hemmed in on every side.

When Teresa was seven, she and her brother Rodrigo decided to implement their desire for martyrdom, running away from home to convert the Muslims. A relative saw them on the road and returned them home. Only a few years later, this youthful piety gave way to frivolity. As a vivacious, attractive teenager, and perhaps acting out some of the drama of the romances she was reading, Teresa engaged in enough flirtatious behavior to cause her father to send her to Our Lady of Grace, an Augustinian convent, for eighteen months. At sixteen she was more than capable of tarnishing the family's honor. An illness in 1532, the first of many, brought her home to recover, after which she decided to enter the Carmelite house of the Encarnation without her father's consent. She took the veil in 1536.

The Encarnation was a popular convent, housing daughters from most of the leading families in Avila. The large numbers (180 women) meant that the Rule was followed carefully by some, indifferently by others. Some wealthy women, including Teresa, came to the convent with an entourage of family members, friends, and servants and had the best quarters and food. Some wealthy nuns held soirées for male friends and family—enjoying music, poetry, and likely good wine. Nuns from less affluent families lived much more poorly.

The nuns were free to come and go; return to family when ill; invite male and female friends to the convent; and often they were called upon to attend to the needs of wealthy patrons and benefactors in their homes for extended periods of time. This portrait clashes sharply with the image of a cloistered convent of enclosure, silence, and prayer and was among the reasons that eventually led Teresa to desire reform.

Another illness in 1538 brought her to her Uncle Pedro's to convalesce, where she read Francisco de Osuna's (c. 1492–1540) *Third Spiritual*

Alphabet with great enthusiasm. Her spiritual life began to deepen and become more authentic. She started thinking of her relationship with God in terms of friendship and love. Later she would describe the presence of God within the human person as a taste of heaven on earth.[5]

After returning to the convent, she went into a coma which resulted in partial paralysis for three years—everyone thought she was dying. But she recovered, speaking with remorse about how she had abandoned prayer for two years in the midst of the pain and depression of illness and indifference. But like her contemporary, Ignatius of Loyola, Teresa used convalescence as a time of spiritual growth. She consulted with the Franciscan Peter of Alcántara and a number of Jesuit spiritual directors, including Francis Borgia, who would later lead the Jesuits. In 1543, Teresa nursed her father until his death in December.

For more than a decade after her father's death, Teresa experienced enormous spiritual growth, including a Lenten experience of Christ suffering on the cross in 1554 and her "spiritual betrothal" in 1556. But in an environment in which exceptional spiritual experiences were suspect, Teresa had to be careful—the idea that her visions might be demonic surfaced first in 1558.

By 1560, Teresa began to act on her vision of a Carmelite reform.[6] A meeting at the Encarnation with a small group of nuns and laywomen who met to talk about prayer produced a desire for a different form of religious life focused on prayer and community. Teresa assumed leadership, but had to confront strong contrary forces within the Order, the town, and Rome—including lawsuits and the threat to withhold absolution for her sins. This was not going to be easy. But the first reformed convent, St. Joseph's, opened in 1562. In this same year, Teresa completed a draft of *The Book of Her Life* and wrote the Constitutions for a reformed Carmel.

Teresa succeeded in enlisting John of the Cross (1567) and Jerónimo Gracián (1572) to help her in the reform of the male side of the Carmelite order. Teresa founded reformed convents in Medina del

Campo, Malagón, Valladolid, Toledo, Salamanca, Seville, and many other cities—seventeen in all.

The forces threatening Teresa's theological and spiritual vision grew. *The Book of Her Life* was submitted to the Inquisition in the 1570s and remained there till after her death, eventually finding a home in the library of Philip II at El Escorial.[7] Not surprisingly, pirated copies circulated and in 1575 the troubled Princess of Eboli denounced Teresa. Discontented nuns in Seville also made complaints against Teresa to the tribunal. At one point, she was ordered to end the reform and confine herself to a convent in Toledo. Complaints against Teresa included: disdain for vocal prayer; personal visions; and excessive interest in mental prayer. But one of Teresa's supporters, Domingo Báñez, wisely sent the book to Madrid where it was given the stamp of approval. Support from influential clergy, the king and his court, and a wide popular following, as well as Teresa's willingness to submit to the Church's judgment, meant that she and her work would survive.

Like Catherine with Italian, Teresa of Avila was one of the first innovators of modern Spanish literature and a creative, independent theological thinker. Her works include *The Book of Her Life; Spiritual Testimonies and Soliloquies; Constitutions and On Making the Visitation; The Way of Perfection; The Interior Castle; Meditations on the Song of Songs;* and *The Book of Her Foundations.* She wrote *The Interior Castle* in 1577, the same year John of the Cross was imprisoned by Carmelites in Toledo who opposed the reform.

By 1580, papal permission was given for the discalced to become an independent province. Teresa became ill again while in Toledo—being constantly on the road in difficult situations took a toll on her health. In 1582, she left Avila for the last time to found a convent in Burgos. On the way home to Avila in September, Teresa's superior discerned that the Duchess of Alba's request for a "holy woman" to be present at the birth of her child should be honored, and she ordered Teresa to go there. Two weeks later, Teresa was dead—on October 4, the feast of St. Francis of Assisi.[8] She was beatified by Pope Paul V in 1614; canonized in 1622 by

Pope Gregory XV; and declared a Doctor of the Church by Pope Paul VI in 1970, the first woman to be so named.

Sixteenth-Century Context

The sixteenth-century in Spain was a period of enormous cultural, intellectual, and literary productivity. Influenced by the Italian Renaissance, Spain came into its own in what is known as the Golden Age of Spanish Literature, which produced exceptional romances, plays, courtly love lyrics, and works of chivalry. Famous names include the poet, Garcilaso de la Vega (1501–1536), playwright Lope de Vega, and Miguel de Cervantes (1547–1616), author of *Don Quixote.*

In addition to a return to the classical masterpieces of Virgil, Horace, Ovid, and Plato, Spaniards were exposed to the northern European humanism of Erasmus of Rotterdam (1466–1536). Humanism advocated study of the Bible in its original languages, the translation of the Bible and Greek and Latin patristic literature into the vernacular, and a flowering of new spiritualities. A prolific writer, Erasmus argued for a gradual, peaceful reform of the Church to which he owed his independent life as a scholar, and whose failings he frequently criticized and satirized. As Spain became more insulated, his thought was suspect and his books banned.

The great religious upheaval of the period involved the Protestant and Roman Catholic Reformations. To understand the historical dynamics of Teresa's life, it is important to note a marked contrast between the first and second halves of the sixteenth century. In the early years of the century, there was a movement that supported Bible reading for everyone (including women and laity). A leading promoter of opening the heights of the spiritual life to women was the learned Spanish Cardinal Ximénez Cisneros (d. 1517). He was a champion of women visionaries and authorized translations into Spanish of many theological and spiritual works.

Small "Bible study" groups met in homes and were often led by women (many of whom were *conversos*) who read and interpreted texts for others.[9] Not unlike the renewal of Vatican II in the twentieth century, this biblical and spiritual awakening was inclusive of all segments in the Church. The windows of the Church opened to recognize the Spirit at work in those who had been considered ineligible for the worlds of interior spirituality and theology.

But the Reformation also brought spiritual unrest and a challenge to the ecclesial monopoly on access to God. The growing number of Christians developing an interior spiritual life threatened to diminish institutional rituals such as sacraments and public prayer. The terms *alhumbrados* and *illuminists* were used to identify and condemn those who engaged in the kind of inner, Spirit-filled, contemplative prayer that drew Teresa closer and closer to God. The response to these new mystical movements included confining women to ever-smaller spheres of influence. Church leaders such as the Dominican Melchior Cano voiced suspicion and hostility, especially toward women.

The Spanish Inquisition, originally created to keep watch on *conversos* tempted to return to Jewish practices, assumed the role of doctrinal watchdog. Vernacular Bibles and spiritual texts were destroyed and women were forbidden to interpret sacred texts or preach or teach in public. In 1529, the holy woman Isabel de la Cruz was sentenced to life in prison, and in 1532, Maria de Cazalla was denounced to the Inquisition. A common complaint against women was their presumption to do theology—contravening the long-standing rule that theology was the exclusive purview of educated clerics. In 1559 the *Index of Forbidden Books* listed writings in the vernacular related to the Bible and mental prayer.

Teresa's theology was born in this dangerous and uncertain theological climate of suspicion and fear.[10] She wisely protested that she was not a "book theologian" (*letrado*), but she did not deny her call to share what the Holy Spirit had taught her. She found ways to encourage mental prayer, even though it was strongly discouraged by Church leaders.

TERESA'S THEOLOGY OF THE HUMAN PERSON

Like the other female Doctors of the Church, Teresa's theology bears the mark of her spiritual journey. That is, a major source for her understanding of the human person was her personal knowledge of coming to know and love God over the course of her life. Teresa did not completely escape the tradition that held the body suspect, but she overcame this view in significant ways. She wrote:

> To be always withdrawn from corporeal things and enkindled in love is the trait of angelic spirits, not of those who live in mortal bodies. It's necessary that we speak to, think about, and become the companions of those who, having had a mortal body, accomplished such great feats for God. How much more is it necessary not to withdraw through one's own efforts from all our good and help, which is the most sacred humanity of our Lord Jesus Christ.[11]

The theological foundation for this positive assessment of embodied human life was Teresa's reverence for Christ's humanity. She refused to accept the teaching that guided people away from Christ's humanity as they reached the upper echelons of the spiritual life. Christ's humanity, including his bodiliness, was never to be left behind. And Christ's body made all human bodies sacred.

Teresa often appealed to experience. It is important to note, however, the significant differences between how Teresa understood human experience and the way we use that term now. Prior to Freud and the evolution of the discipline of psychology, experience was not understood in an anthropocentric way, as in "what did you do today"? Rather, the human person was viewed and valued primarily as an image of God. The perspective was theocentric.

Teresa was not interested in her daily experiences per se but only inasmuch as they provided a mirror or window into God. Her regard for the humanity of Christ and her understanding of the human person were two sides of the same coin. In addition to her relationship with God, Teresa also recommended spiritual books, describing them as important aids to prayer. When vernacular books were prohibited, she wrote her own books to aid her sisters in their spiritual journeys. A distinctive note of her anthropology is that she steadfastly included women as well as men as having access to the higher reaches of contemplative prayer. God in Christ desired to dwell in everyone, not just men or those with theological or clerical credentials.

Rowan Williams also underscores the importance, for her theology, of Teresa's identity as a "displaced person." Her theology emerges from her experience "as a woman and a Jewess, undergoing ecstatic experiences, and claiming certain kinds of authority, at a time when any one of these would have guaranteed her not being taken seriously in Church and society, except as a threat and a pollutant." She negotiated her life "in an almost wholly suspicious environment."[12] These circumstances led her to see and insist on an inclusive human potential for holiness.[13]

Teresa's adherence to what she saw as the truth inevitably raised the issue of authority. She must have been acutely aware that Church leaders would raise questions about an uneducated woman departing from the theological status quo. After describing the four waters of grace, she wrote: "I should certainly like to have a great deal of authority in this matter so that I might be believed."[14]

Teresa's theology offers an elevated, enticing vision of the human capacity for God. At the outset of *The Interior Castle,* she wrote: "It is a shame and unfortunate that through our own fault we don't understand ourselves or know who we are—that is loved by God."[15] Spiritual self-knowledge includes both positive and negative qualities. It does not mean simply gathering information about ourselves, but seeing ourselves truly in the light of God which brings about humility, repentance, and joy.

Teresa knew about the endless "ticker tape" that kept her in illusion—worrying about what others thought of her, anxiety about trivial matters, reliving past hurts, and rehearsing future arguments. She knew about the subtlety and complexity of the devil's wiles aimed at keeping her tied up in knots and full of self-regard. Part of Teresa's genius was to sort out the confusion between self-knowledge and self-preoccupation and marvel that, in spite of human weakness, God dwells within, calling the desiring soul to intimate love. "By seeing God we see more clearly what we are—muddled, distracted, but in motion toward the love of God."[16]

Teresa's theology may seem individualistic on the surface but it is deeply communal in its orientation. Her small, enclosed community served as a workshop where she learned how to love others. It is true that the relationship between theology and community is quite different for us, given that our "community" encompasses the entire world with which we are in daily touch through media coverage. But Teresa's theological wisdom provides a map for ways to be in loving relationship with others, how to be faithful about daily tasks, and how to attend to the concrete, historical setting out of which theology is done.

Friendship is central to her theology of the human person and to how she saw relationship with God. Once again, Teresa escaped dualism. For her, human and divine friendships informed and shed light on each other. Her insights about friendship and love have wide application from a family to a corporate boardroom. The "other" is not "hell" as Sartre would have it, but the royal, usually difficult, path to knowledge and love of God.

Lovable and Capable: A Positive Anthropology

Teresa gradually discovered that her identity entailed something "incomparably more precious" than she could have imagined. She wrote: "Let's not imagine that we are hollow inside."[17] Rather the soul is like "a paradise where the Lord says He finds His delight."[18] She acknowledged that it is almost impossible to understand our dignity and beauty because it is like God's. But society had schooled her to sell herself short. "I understood well that I had a soul. But what this soul deserved and who dwelt within it I did not understand because I had covered my eyes with the vanities of the world."[19] But then she discovered that, without forcing our will, God gradually enlarges the soul's capacity if we but clear away the debris.[20]

Teresa's firsthand discovery of the human potential for God turned her into a cheerleader for all Christians. She did not want the sisters or any Christian to settle for mediocrity.[21] And she was convinced that this is also God's deepest desire for us. Teresa asks that we use our reason to become dissatisfied with a slow, plodding approach to God. She knew well what it meant to plod, literally and spiritually. She spent a good part of her life sloshing through drenching rain and slippery, wet mud to found reformed convents. She asks her readers: "Does it seem to you, daughters, that if we could go from one land to another in eight days, it would be good to take a year through wind, snow, rain, and bad roads?"[22] Thérèse of Lisieux makes a similar point, using the metaphor of an elevator as superior to trudging up stairs. For Teresa, the mud symbolized fear, worries, timidity, and extreme circumspection.

Teresa wondered why we do not notice that we are rich. She wrote: "How can anyone benefit and share his gifts lavishly if he doesn't understand that he is rich?… It is impossible because of our nature for someone who doesn't know he is favored by God to have enthusiasm for great things."[23] This insight was hard won. To begin, the pecking order of identity in sixteenth-century Spain was enormous—lineage, nationality, religious background. Teresa turned this oppressive order on its head. She changed the rules, focusing instead on "the precious things that can be found in this soul, or who dwells within it, or its high value."[24] Without compromising the truth that God is infinitely greater than creation, Teresa wants her readers to know that they have direct access to God and the potential to be one with the three divine persons.

This insight into the value of the human person was not automatic. Teresa had to overcome personal demons—her youthful need to be loved and admired, and to please others. She knew she was attractive and desirable on many levels, but in sixteenth-century Spanish culture, what was attractive about women also made them dangerous. To be desirable was not the same as to be lovable in religious terms. This all changed when she imagined herself before the needy Christ of Gethsemane, and for the first time, saw "herself as needed and welcomed simply as a human companion, as someone whose mere presence might be a grace or comfort in the suffering of another."[25]

Teresa is not alone in her anxiety about being acceptable. Many Christians without a clue about their own beauty as images of God sell themselves short, remaining in the rather dull outer regions of the castle, oblivious to what might lie ahead. But she reminds the reader to remain steadfast, because "God does not deny Himself to anyone who perseveres" providing for each person the courage, bit by bit, to reach the goal.[26]

Although Teresa had extraordinary experiences of God, she taught that ordinary prayer, like an intimate conversation with a friend, was available to all. All that was necessary was to bring one's full self to God, in weakness as well as strength. Teresa also valued the Eucharist when Christ comes close in the eating and drinking of his body and blood. Her deep desire, and one of the reasons she wrote theology, was to convince her readers of this truth and embolden them to open themselves to this destiny.

Teresa imagined the soul with its goal of union with God in Christ, as the inmost center of a castle, an architectural structure Teresa saw all around her. The castle is large and has lots of rooms—a place of infinite variety and richness—like the many mansions of the Gospel.[27] She acknowledged that not everyone would be called to the specific way she proposed, and this does not matter, since the point is not a certain form of meditation but love.[28] Teresa speaks to our pluralistic age when she acknowledges how many different paths there are. Within the context of the doctrines of creation, incarnation and Holy Spirit, each Christian must pursue her or his own unique way.[29] "Here all three Persons communicate themselves to the soul, speak to it, and explain those words of the Lord in the Gospel: that He and the Father and the Holy Spirit will come to dwell with the soul that loves Him and keeps His commandments."[30]

GRACE: WHO DOES WHAT?

Following in the footsteps of Augustine, Teresa emphasized the gifted nature of union with God. We do not reach God by pulling ourselves up by our own bootstraps. And yet she wrote: "Works are what the Lord wants!" That is, God wants us to look on the suffering of others with compassion and act to relieve it.[31] Teresa uses the metaphor of watering a garden to imagine the grace of God and the human contributions to this journey. Like John the Baptist, Christians prepare the way for the graces that God desires to offer all her beloved creatures. These include meditation, the faithful practice of the virtues and, above all, love of neighbor.

In her *Life*, Teresa presented her famous description of the "four waters." At the beginning, the person seeking to pray must cultivate the barren soil of a garden that God has already weeded and seeded. The task is to water the garden (develop virtues) so that the Lord will take delight and find joy there.[32] There are four ways to water the garden: draw water from the well, which takes a lot of work; turn the crank of the water wheel and send it through aqueducts, which takes less effort; use water that flows from a river or stream, which does a much better job without much labor; or, best of all, just let the rain fall on the garden, which requires no elbow grease at all.[33] On the one hand, God's grace is everything. On the other hand, water must be drawn by faithfully engaging in reflection, works of charity, spiritual reading, and conversations. The disposition of confident, open, watchful waiting is required, since the spirit ascends only at God's behest.

At the second water, or prayer of quiet, the ratio of human labor to divine gift shifts, making grace more clearly manifest to the soul.[34] The will takes center stage as the person consents to becoming a prisoner of a loving God. The virtues flourish more easily, and even if one responds to these graces with ingratitude, God's mercies prevail. The greater the fault, the greater the forgiveness and love.[35] Some continue to practice mental prayer, but in the growing state of quiet, it takes more and more effort to speak. Eschewing consolation, the soul desires only to help Christ carry his cross.

At the third water, all that is required is to direct the flow of water. At this stage, Christ practically becomes the gardener himself. The faculties experience a kind of sleep, what Teresa described as "a glorious foolishness, a heavenly madness where the true wisdom is learned; and it is for the soul a most delightful way of enjoying."[36] The disquiet is "delightful" and the soul is beside itself, desiring to be "all tongues" and "to cry out praises."[37]

In the end, the fourth, superabundant water "soaks and saturates this entire garden." Grace gradually causes the soul to expand—over a lifetime or in a nanosecond—culminating in ecstasy. Work becomes glory filled with joy and consolation. It is the flame that shoots above the fire. It is water that paradoxically causes the fire to increase.[38] The body swoons, unable to breathe or function.[39] The proof of God's magnanimity is that union is given even in this life.[40] The fruit is exquisite tenderness and joyous tears. The very idea of union with God is mindboggling, stopping the intellect in its tracks.

To compensate, Teresa found herself speaking "absurdities." Although her theology favors the kataphatic way to God (finding God in the world—nature, images, books, art, etc.),[41] at this point, Teresa turns to apophatic theology (the way of negation) to express the inexpressible— "there is an understanding by not understanding."[42]

Teresa's garden metaphor can help ward off the temptation to think about grace as a "thing" or as a competition between humanity and God. In this latter view, human activity—to develop theological understanding, to practice prayer and virtue, to work for justice— is wrongly seen as a diminishment of God's utterly gratuitous grace. Teresa's four waters metaphor moves us away from a scale that measures weight in inverse proportion, replacing it with one that recognizes intimate collaboration—100 percent God and 100 percent human. As she wrote, "One water draws down the other."[43] Teresa emphasizes the importance of fidelity and perseverance in prayer, but not as a cause of God's favors. God showers grace as God pleases, but this does not obviate the need to be faithful servants day in and day out.[44]

God revealed to Teresa that true humility is "to know what you can do and what I can do."[45] As participants in God's divine nature, human beings are partners and collaborators with God.[46] It is their nature to be drawn into the intimate circle of the Trinity. The soul is not lowly, God told Teresa, "for it is made in My image."[47] Teresa had no patience for anyone who refused to believe that God can give great favors to us—a refusal that "has indeed closed the door to receiving them."[48]

Sin and Conversion

Teresa learned how sin negates or blocks all the divine gifts God intends for us. And without God's gifts, our nature is dead.[49] Sin is like putting a black cloth over the dazzling brilliance of the sun, that is, the divine presence at the heart of existence.[50] In the outer rooms of the Castle—indeed throughout the entire journey—the soul is to seek self-knowledge. "Knowing ourselves is something so important that I wouldn't want any relaxation ever in this regard, however high you may have climbed into the heavens."[51]

As noted above, the key to self-knowledge is knowledge of God. When we keep our eye on God, we discover that we are both lowly/sinful (humility) and made in God's image (graced). By focusing on God, the soul avoids illusion (something Teresa abhorred) and avoids getting mired in the pettiness and misery of our sinfulness. How boring our preoccupation with sin must be to a God who desires that we become free of self-preoccupation, that the waters of grace flow freely, unstopped by the mud of "fears, faintheartedness, and cowardice."[52]

We need to interpret Teresa's references to her sinfulness on two levels. First, we know that she used rhetoric to convince powerful clergy that she was not overstepping the limited boundaries assigned to women in the Church. She needed to protect herself against accusations that she was an uppity woman who presumed to teach theology. Acknowledging her sinfulness and abject status in the Church was one way to do this.

But on another level we encounter her authentic awakening to the truth of her appalling sin.

In different ways, Catherine of Siena and Teresa awaken to sin in the face of God's tremendous love. Teresa's experience of unmerited, gratuitous love opened her eyes to the ways she devalued, manipulated, and diminished herself and others. She became attuned to the subtle ways in which her desires for goodness and reform could be tainted by selfishness. She wrote: "I was living an extremely burdensome life, because in prayer I understood more clearly my faults."[53] She wrestled with the tension between external appearance and internal reality; with the social and spiritual mores of her time; with self-deception and illusion; and with the Church, her confessors, and her nuns. Her world constantly reminded her of the wily and dangerous work of the devil.

But the greatest sin for her was her own ignorance and ingratitude in the face of so great a love.[54] She deeply regretted what she viewed as twenty years of mediocrity and indifference—at one point, in 1543–1544, she had stopped praying altogether. Teresa gradually came to experience sin as also a blessing or "happy fault" because it gave her yet another reason to praise God's infinite mercies. Instead of despair, the truth of her sinfulness led her to gratitude and an ever more intimate relationship with God. On still another level, she realized that sin did not matter, since God was free to offer divine gifts to anyone—sinner or saint—in order to manifest God's glory.[55]

While Teresa identified with the conversion of Augustine, I think hers had a broader arc, spanning her entire life. There were obvious highlights, such as her experience before the suffering Christ and her mystical marriage. But over the course of many years, she moved from a more abstract knowledge that we are all sinners (see John 8:7; 1 John 1:8) to a piercing insight into what can only be described as her colossal indifference to God's exquisite, unqualified love. The heart of her conversion was her discovery that she was embraced by God, always, just as she was, in her totality. This new self was at last freed from her desperate need to be liked and accepted by others. Teresa also applied what she learned about her personal sin to society, challenging the harmful, empty ways in which Spain's elite related to each other, offering a radically different basis for human interaction.

After she entered the convent, God gifted her with a sense of happiness and joy that amazed her and stayed with her.[56] But she also labored under an atonement model of salvation, prominent at the time, that held that the soul needed to suffer and make sacrifices in order to gain God's favor. By paying attention to what God was working in her, Teresa realized that the status quo did not work for her: dwelling on her sins, ruminating on how much she owed God, worrying about what would lead her to heaven or hell, or forcing herself to think about Christ's sufferings only depressed her.[57] Gradually she saw the truth of the ways her weaknesses blocked her from God's gifts. Thus, she inspires her readers not to blindly "buy into" what they are told about sin (and its undoing) but to discover in God's presence the truth of sin, including its nuances and subtle self-deceptions.

In the midst of these agonies, Teresa left open a window that allowed God to work a new thing in her. "O Lord of my soul! How can I extol the favors You gave me during these years! And how at the time when I offended You most You quickly prepared me with an extraordinary repentance to taste Your favors and gifts!… With wonderful gifts you punished my sins!"[58] Teresa admitted that it was harder to accept gifts than punishment, which may be true for many Christians. The mirror of human spiritual capacity is a God of gifts—*contentos* are gifts that God offers for a job well done; *gustos* are gifts given gratis out of God's infinitely generous love. God leads sinners toward conversion, toward a genuine awareness of sin, and toward a willingness to be born on the wings of divine love and forgiveness.

We Are Made to Be with and for Each Other

It may seem surprising that an enclosed contemplative would place so much emphasis on love of neighbor and service to the world.[59] And yet our three regular female monastics who are Doctors of the Church (and also Catherine) envisioned a theology whose bottom line is love of others. Theirs is a communitarian theology. We are in this castle together. Teresa and Thérèse of Lisieux felt the loss of being blocked from public ministry, and they expressed envy toward those who had the "freedom to cry out and announce the news abroad about who this great God of hosts is."[60] They do not understand intimacy with God as a private, exclusive relationship but as a gift given to benefit others in active, compassionate love to heal the world's suffering.[61] Both were conscious of the Church's missionary efforts and desirous of supporting them through prayer.

For Teresa, external works were inseparable from the heights of mystical love. Commenting on the Song of Songs 2:5 (Sustain me with raisins, / refresh me with apples; / for I am faint with love), she wrote: "I understand by these words that the soul is asking to perform great works in the service of the Lord and its neighbor...Martha and Mary never fail to work together when the soul is in this state."[62] Teresa has a distinctive interpretation of the Great Commandment to love God and love the neighbor. She wrote: "We cannot know whether or not we love God, although there are strong indications for recognizing that we do love Him; but we can know whether we love our neighbor."[63] Thus, if we are successfully caring for others, we can presume that our love for God is flourishing.

We have noted how important friendship is in Teresa's theological vision. She encouraged her readers to seek out others who practice prayer.[64] She saw sharing conversation about the joys and trials of the spiritual life as a fitting way to nurture friendship with God.[65] She knew the comfort of finding others who were also spiritually wounded and ill, but nevertheless willing to help each other.[66] Even though friendships are far from perfect, they remain a means through which God works good in souls.

The geography of her friendship with the Lord was a reverse image of the deforming aspects of the social mores of her time in which power, position, and prestige dominated. Part of what it means to be a Christian is to desire holiness for those we love. Teresa suggests that spiritual seekers joyfully assume responsibility for the spiritual progress of others—not in an arrogant or preachy way, but because of a genuine desire that our friends love God as fully as possible. She trusted in the "mercy of God, who never fails to repay anyone who has taken Him for a friend. For mental prayer, in my opinion is nothing else than an intimate sharing between friends."[67] It might be fruitful to ponder the specific ways in which twenty-first-century culture encourages deformed relationships. It also may not occur to us to include spiritual well-being as a central element in our close relationships, but Teresa clearly thought otherwise. She nudges us to ask: What does it truly mean to love family and friends "in Christ"?

Teresa's Theology Today

Teresa of Avila offers many points of contact for twenty-first-century Christians. The long list: Her "theological insight, her political acumen, her sheer tenacity…her self-awareness, her vision of community life as the realm of God in microcosm, her love of the Church, her realism about human relationships, and perhaps mostly her sense of the close friendship offered by God, all inform our sense of her as a saint, a person whose life and witness point to God in our world."[68] The short list: "Pray and serve."[69] Teresa's theology arose out of prayer, which produced a clarity of vision and knowledge that does not fit neatly into the standard categories of systematic theology. Instead she left us a fuller legacy about God's identity, human existence, and the relationship between the two.

Teresa lived in a hierarchically rigid Catholic culture that disdained women, Jews, Protestants, and mystics. The freshness and depth of her theology reveal not only how she survived, but even flourished, in the midst of hostility and suspicion. But she had supporters as well. In 1627, on the occasion of her nomination as copatron of Spain (with Santiago de Compostela), Jesuit Rodrigo Niño preached: "Sanctity in women usually consists in being quiet, obeying, staying in a corner and forgetting about oneself; O new miracle and rare prodigy! Not by keeping quiet, but by speaking, teaching and writing; not only by obeying, but by ordering, commanding, governing; not by observing enclosure but by traveling, disputing."[70] Her vision of the human person as capable of hearing and following God's invitation to friendship and intimate love enabled her to stand her ground.

The hierarchies of the sixteenth century—king, nobility, "pure bloods," and men, followed by workers, women, and the poor—are not that different from those of the twenty-first and both equally destructive. Co-opting the very language of hierarchy, Teresa spoke of grace as a power that overturns every hierarchy. A humble God receives everyone, even the most lowly and despised.[71] Teresa was able to sort the wheat from the chaff of how the Christian tradition was being lived around her. She noticed when the status quo thwarted genuine freedom and spiritual maturity, human qualities we continue to prize.

In defending mental prayer against detractors, Teresa told the sisters not to be afraid as fear destroys the spiritual life.[72] Any intimidation of the spirit that suggests the soul is not capable of great blessing is to be rejected.[73] Teresa was not talking about the gift of "fear of the Lord" that acknowledges God's infinite power, wisdom, and goodness. Rather, she refers to fear that is destructive and paralyzing. The Spain in which Teresa lived was riddled with fear, a feeling that is also rampant in the twenty-first century. How would Teresa counsel us to resist our daily social conditioning to fear for our safety, to worry about possessions—fears that lead inevitably to a sense of entitlement and self-preoccupation? Those around Teresa feared new spiritual developments; they feared the king and capricious nobles; they feared the Inquisition. And Teresa had her own fears to overcome—losing her reputation, having people reject her, fear of evil spirits, and self-deception.

But Teresa faced her fears head-on, unlike so many in the Church whom Teresa experienced as pusillanimous, small-minded, and self-protective. Her theology of the human person teaches us to "go for the gold." She counsels us to desire with abandon because this God might very likely say "yes" to everything. Teresa saw the human person as one who should entertain no limits in a relationship with God, because to limit our desires is to limit a limitless God.[74]

Teresa sensed in some of her spiritual directors a fear of getting into trouble or of making a poor judgment call which might ruin their reputations. She not only suffered from this personally, but she was angry at their willingness to settle for mediocrity. She was scandalized by their refusal to engage in, or support, mental prayer which she saw as the entry, the journey, and the culmination of life with God. It was blasphemy to allow either petty or genuine fears to smother the freedom of the children of God.

Teresa's determination echoes the stories in the Gospels about women who would not back down in their approach to Jesus: the widow and the unjust judge (Luke 18:1–8) and the Canaanite woman who sought a cure for her daughter (Matthew 15:22–28; Mark 7:24–30). God worked with Teresa's focused, insistent personality by rewarding her with gifts beyond her imagining. Human beings are the beneficiaries of a God whose greatest delight is in giving presents to those who approach.

Building on her experience and her insight into the Scriptures, Teresa challenges us to examine whether our relationship with God is as dogged and faithful as it might be. Twentieth-century British poet T.S. Eliot captures this aspect of Teresa's theology: "There is only the trying. The rest is not our business."[75] She says to those who want to travel on this road of loving friendship with God: "They must have a great and very resolute determination to persevere until reaching the end, come what may, happen what may, whatever work is involved, whatever criticism arises, whether they arrive or whether they die on the road, or even if they don't have courage for the trials that are on it, or if the whole world collapses."[76] It would be interesting to compile a list of rationalizing obstacles parallel to the ones Teresa mentions: "there are dangers"; "so-and-so went astray"; "this other one was deceived"; "it's not for women"; "the Our Father and the Hail Mary are sufficient."[77]

Determination follows upon desire. How much do we want from God? The state and intensity of our desire fuels perseverance. In the end, for Teresa, the enemy was anything that leads us to be satisfied with rote, routine, mindless prayer. No matter what kind of prayer we choose, it should be characterized by presence, awareness, intentionality, and above all truth. In mysterious ways divine truth engraved upon her being a sure knowledge of the truth—about how her identity and that of the world mirrored the identity of God, who taught her to "walk in truth before Truth itself."[78] Being a human being (and not a zombie) means that we should be "at home" and present to ourselves and God when we pray and live. It should be real and true—the way we would want any important relationship to be.

Through many dark and stormy seas, Teresa arrived at an under-standing of the human person that was deeply theological, reflecting the very being of God. Her Christian anthropology provides a needed and blessed complement to contemporary self-understandings that depend too exclusively on psychology and economics. Her way leads from narrow, petty self-preoccupation to a self-transcendence that opens us to the neighbor in need and to the universe. She helps us imagine the very marrow of our existence as the dwelling place of the Trinity, and, like the Trinity, we are made to live in relationship: companionship, nurture, service, compassion, enjoyment, challenge, struggle, and love. Teresa wrote to convince us that God really wants us as we are. She asks us to trust that God will steadily expand our entire being to accommo-date the divine presence.

Teresa wants us to be in awe of the truth that human beings are the space in which God becomes most real and present to us and to our world.[79] Her theology has concrete, practical effects in the world. Teresa would endorse our twenty-first-century attempts to broaden this theology to include care for our threatened ecosystems. Karl Rahner champions her human skills: "The fact that her desire for penance did not lessen her appreciation of good roast partridge and that she was also an incomparably worldly-wise organizer and diplomat...these are also things which make her mysticism particularly sympathetic to us today."[80] Teresa laments any primary understanding of ourselves and our capacities as other than as image of God—an image with as many faces as there are human beings. Because there is no cookie-cutter recipe, God provides many mansions, allowing each person to pay reverent attention to the God within. We are to trust and test what God brings about in the soul, especially when it subverts the status quo.

Inner personal transformation leads to ecclesial and social action for justice. According to Teresa, when it comes to God and the human person, we simply think too small.[81] Our true identity is to be a dwelling place for the Trinity and servant to the world. Teresa's penetrating knowledge into the nature of relationship encompasses and joins the world and God.

In the seventh mansions, she twice notes that God told her that "it was time that she consider as her own what belonged to Him and that He would take care of what was hers."[82] And we can certainly apply to ourselves Teresa's humorous comment to the sisters: "I think it will be a consolation for you to delight in this interior castle since without permission from the prioress [or anyone else] you can enter and take a walk through it at any time."[83]

THEOLOGICAL REFLECTION

- Recall a moment when you experienced being beside yourself with delight and had a spontaneous urge to praise God. It might be as weighty as the birth of a child or as simple as a brisk, fall day; a moving story or piece of music; or the smile of a child. In this moment how do you experience yourself as a human being? As a child of God?

- Have you ever put on a raincoat (or not) and gone outside in a downpour? Abandoned yourself to the rain, banished all concern about wet clothes, or getting a cold, or tracking mud into the house? This is a literal way to get the sense of grace as Teresa describes it in her theology. If rain is not your thing, think of alternate experiences to sense the utter abundance of God's love.

- How would you rate yourself in terms of your spiritual desires and your perseverance during dry or difficult times? What can Teresa teach you about going for the gold, about not giving up?

- Make a list of connections that you make (or would like to make) between Christ's humanity and your own humaness, the world, and the cosmos.

- What gives authority to your own theological and spiritual voices?

CHAPTER FIVE

Thérèse of Lisieux (1873–1897)
Theology of the Cross

As a Carmelite, Thérèse of Lisieux would have known the writings of Teresa of Avila and John of the Cross. While Thérèse benefited from this rich Carmelite tradition, she created her own unique spiritual version in the context of her life and nineteenth-century France. Even though Thérèse is closer to us in time, there remain many elements of her life and theology that feel foreign. She spent her life in the tightly enclosed religious environments of her family and the Lisieux Carmel. Her writing style has been described as childish, sentimental, syrupy, trivial, and irrelevant to the harsh realities of life in the twenty-first century.[1] Some even see her as a negative model for strong, intelligent women who dedicate themselves to family life and maintain demanding jobs in the public arena.[2]

But attention to her words and to the many rigorous and thoughtful interpretations of her work tells a different story. It is not without reason that on World Mission Sunday, October 19, 1997, in St. Peter's Square, John Paul II declared Thérèse of Lisieux a Doctor of the universal Church. A distinctive mark of Thérèse's way is its emphasis on "the little and the humble" (Luke 10:21–22; Matthew 11:25–30)—traits that appear to be in tension with the lofty title of "Doctor." The originality and style of her theological legacy is markedly different from a master of doctrine such as Thomas Aquinas. But her contemplative, Spirit-inspired insight into the Scriptures, her integration of experience and doctrinal truth, and her ability to teach in creative and inspiring ways certainly qualify her to be named Doctor of the Church.

Life and Works

The story of Thérèse of Lisieux is well known to many.[3] She grew up in a comfortable home with her parents and four sisters, all of whom entered religious life. Both her mother, Zélie Guérin, and her father, Louis Martin, grew up in devout families. Both felt called to religious life, but both were denied acceptance when they applied. Zélie prayed: "Lord, since I am not worthy to be your bride, I will enter the married state in order to fulfill Your holy will. I beg of You to give me many children and to let them all be consecrated to you." The vocational desires of the parents would indeed be fulfilled by their children. Zélie's sister Marie Louise also became a Visitation nun.

Louis and Zélie were married at the Church of Notre Dame in 1858. On the day of their wedding, they went to visit Zélie's sister at the Visitation Convent. Later Zélie wrote to her daughter Pauline that she could not stop crying because she wanted so much to be a nun with her sister. Since Louis also desired religious life, he was able to comfort her and this shared attitude brought them closer together. Later, Zélie wrote letters to her sister in which they spoke to each other of "a mysterious angelic world, above the mire of this earth."

At first, Louis and Zélie decided to live as celibates, an arrangement that lasted ten months until a confessor helped them embrace their call to have children. The children who arrived brought them great joy: Marie Louise, Marie Pauline, Marie Léonie, and Marie Hélène (who died at five years). Zélie then gave birth to two sons who died shortly after birth. Next were Marie-Céline, Melanie-Thérèse (who died in her first year), and on January 2, 1873, Marie-Françoise-Thérèse was born.

Louis was a watchmaker and Zélie founded a successful business creating Alençon lace that provided their fledgling family with a comfortable existence. But they always made room for religious activity. Charitable works, personal prayer, daily Mass, and pilgrimages were at the center of their family life. Various members of the Martin family suffered from ill health. This included Thérèse, who was sent to a wet nurse for a year because of poor health and also suffered bouts of melancholy when she was little. Her sister Léonie was described as a moody child, less gifted than her sisters, and a challenge to raise. Perhaps she was simply reacting against the stifling atmosphere of French Victorian piety.

Zélie battled sadness and scruples and, in the end, died from breast cancer in 1877 at age forty-five. After her death the family moved from Alençon to Lisieux to be closer to Zélie's brother Isidore, his wife, Céline, and their daughters, Jeanne and Marie (who also later joined Carmel). As a young girl, Thérèse survived a severe bout of nerves and an extended period in which she was tormented with scruples, constantly worrying about her sinfulness. The smallest transgression brought on bouts of tears. Thérèse described this mental and spiritual state as "torture."

But the record also reveals a family with bonds of deep love and care. Thérèse was attached to her mother, who remembered Thérèse stroking her face and hugging her. They had the means to travel and engage in activities that brought joy. Thérèse described her early childhood as one that was full of warmth and affection—she was showered with loving embraces and smiles by those around her. At home until age eight under the tutelage of her older sisters, Thérèse then spent five years as a day student at a nearby Benedictine school. Although her teachers found her bright, she struggled with fitting in and being away from family. Thérèse described these years as the "saddest of my life."

We also know that her conservative French Roman Catholic community was concerned about sheltering young daughters from the anticlerical and secular strains in the broader culture. Thérèse and her classmates would have had a restricted reading list, and many of the texts they did read were expurgated. Thérèse notes as well that her Father did not allow the Martin girls to read newspapers. Eventually she returned home and received instruction from a tutor. Thérèse stated that book knowledge was never helpful to her—but she also noted an early interest in science and consulted several biographies of Joan of Arc in preparation for the plays she would write about this famous French woman.

The intensely religious atmosphere of the Martin home led to religious vocations for all the children. First Pauline entered Carmel; six years later, Marie joined her; then Thérèse when she was fifteen; and finally Céline, who had stayed home to care for their father during his final illness. After several failed attempts, Léonie too ended up as a sister of the Visitation. Thérèse saw herself as "a child destined by God to be, by means of prayer and sacrifice, an 'apostle of apostles'"—a title long associated with Mary Magdalene.

Thérèse received the habit on January 10, 1889, and after only nine years in the Lisieux Carmel, died of tuberculosis on September 30, 1897. She was twenty-four. There was a dramatic change in Thérèse during the last eighteen months of her life. She endured a severe test of faith in which her belief in an afterlife evaporated, leaving her in a kind of darkness that caused her great suffering. With a rapidity rare in the Church, Pope Pius XI beatified her in 1923 and canonized her on May 17, 1925. Her parents were beatified on October 19, 2008.

Thérèse experienced changes over the course of her short life. Two notable conversions can be noted. The first was on Christmas Eve in 1886 when an impatient remark from her father about her childish needs provoked her to leave behind her infantile touchiness and recover the spiritual strength she had lost when her mother died. She began a new chapter of her life, temporarily relieved of the heavy burdens of sadness and guilt. She wrote that charity entered her heart, and she felt a need to forget herself.

At the end of her life, she was painfully transformed by a kind of stripping that tested her faith and led to her mature theological reflections. But we can trace a broader arc of conversion that encompasses her whole life. She begins as a scrupulous, judgmental, petulant individual and ends in utter simplicity and loving surrender.

Thérèse's life was marked by tensions and contradictions. She grew up in a bourgeois world of ease, comfort, status, and snobbism that she ended up rejecting. Thérèse was both spiritually audacious and childlike. She wanted to be noticed yet invisible. She craved affection yet wanted to be despised. She had a strong will but sought submission and nothingness. Illness and a nervous condition made her frail and weak, but she maintained a determined spirit. She described herself as a prisoner of Carmel and yet saw herself as a citizen of the world exercising a kind of radical freedom in love.

She and her sisters grew up in what we might call a matriarchal family. We know that their father, Louis, gave up his work as a clock-maker to join his wife, Zélie, in her very successful lace business. Zélie resembled women today who do it all—a breadwinner who also gave herself to the physical, psychological, and spiritual needs of her family. Her spirituality included keeping track of good deeds and self-sacrifice that seems excessive—an understanding of a demanding God that Thérèse eventually left behind. In addition, Zélie was ill with cancer. When she died, her brother, not M. Martin, assumed legal responsibility for the Martin girls.

Although Thérèse was only four and a half when Zélie died, it is hard not to imagine that Zélie's witness and memory provided a rare alternative to the more common patriarchal pattern of nineteenth-century conservative French Catholics. Zélie provided a strong, loving, competent model of womanhood that must have influenced her five daughters in many ways.

Most people who know the writings of Thérèse are familiar with her three-part autobiography, *Story of a Soul,* which she began in January 1895.[4] But she also wrote 54 poems, 21 prayers, 266 extant letters, eight plays written for feast day celebrations, and her last conversations.[5] Her sister Pauline and some others recorded Thérèse's last conversations which some scholars do not regard as a reliably accurate rendering of Thérèse's own thoughts.[6]

Nineteenth-Century Context

To understand the France in which Thérèse lived, it is necessary to examine the forces unleashed a hundred years earlier. The aftermath of the Revolution of 1789 was bloody, violent, and long-lived. The basic struggle was between two forms of government—the long-established monarchy and the vision of a more democratic republicanism. A new progressive urban middle class confronted a more rural feudal culture that sided with the status quo of an empowered, privileged aristocracy.

In addition to economic factors (a gap between rich and poor; abysmal conditions of workers; drought and crop failure), new ideas in politics, culture, the role of religion and the place of women were emerging. In the span of only twenty-five years, France moved from an absolute monarchy to a constitutional monarchy, to various forms of republicanism, the Napoleonic Empire, and back to monarchy under the Bourbons by 1815. After additional revolutions in 1830 and 1848, it was only in 1879—a century after the initial Revolution—that France was finally and firmly established as a republic.

Roman Catholicism suffered enormous losses during this period. Identified with the wealth and privilege of the monarchy, the Church had amassed enormous financial resources enjoyed by bishops at the expense of impoverished parish priests. Some bishops had become cynical nonbelievers, succumbing to growing secular forces. The Revolution of 1789 brought virulent anti-clericalism, violence, and destruction, culminating in the Reign of Terror. The execution of sixteen Carmelites on July 17, 1794, would have been part of the collective memory of the sisters at the Lisieux Carmel.[7] The conflict between revolutionaries and the monarchy deeply affected attitudes toward religion and the Roman Catholic Church which, for the most part, took the side of monarchy and aristocracy. To many Catholics, the Revolution meant terror, and republicanism, injustice. In turn, supporters of the Revolution viewed the Church as the enemy. Clergy, religious, and loyal laity were persecuted, exiled, and killed; Church property was confiscated; monasteries disappeared. In 1830, there was a new wave of anti-clericalism that saw the Church as the foe of freedom.

The revolutionary threat to the French monarchy affected all the other monarchies in Europe, producing a long series of military engagements between France and Italy, Austria, England, Russia, and Prussia. The

Franco-Prussian war of 1870–1871, in which France was subjected to the humiliating loss of Alsace-Lorraine and the siege of Paris, involved the Martin family directly.[8] Many local men were sent to fight and, without proper training, suffered terrible injury and loss. The Martins' town was captured and nine soldiers were billeted in their home before peace was again established. In the first election after the siege of Paris, a majority of conservatives were elected, causing a revolt in the form of the Commune. The violence on both sides was chilling. The Commune shot the archbishop and fifty-three clerics. The government violently suppressed the uprising during the week of May 22–28, 1871, called "Bloody Week."

In 1870, the Kingdom of Italy, supported by France, occupied Rome. Other losses to the Church included the right to appoint bishops and the gradual removal of the Church from public education in France. Eventually a secular France with a strict separation of Church and state was established. Amid this turmoil, the Martin family would have located themselves squarely on the side of the monarchy and against what was perceived as republican secularization, anticlericalism, and de-Christianization. On their pilgrimage to Rome with their Father, Thérèse and Céline would have witnessed this tension firsthand in the form of anti-Church protests and the aftermath of the looting of convents. In France, pilgrimages were seen not only as religious observances but also as pro-monarchist demonstrations. At one point, Monsieur Martin offered Fr. Delatroette, the parish priest at St. Jacques and superior of the Carmel, a hiding place in their home at Les Buissonnets (the little bushes), perhaps fearing a recurrence of the Reign of Terror.[9]

After the Revolution of 1848, Roman Catholics took diverse approaches. Some sought to adapt the faith to the contemporary world. Others advocated submission to papal leadership and the reclamation of the Church's rights. A structural response to secularization and the social upheaval of the period was the declaration of papal infallibility at the First Vatican Council in 1868–1870, called by Pius IX. Later, realizing that secularization was clearly established, Pope Leo XIII (1878–1903) unsuccessfully urged Catholics to embrace the Republic. He saw that efforts to evangelize would be jeopardized without a working relationship with the French people.

During Thérèse's lifetime, Leo XIII also addressed the plight of workers in his famous encyclical *Rerum Novarum,* providing a lasting foundation for Catholic social teaching. On her pilgrimage to Rome, Thérèse and her family had a meeting with Leo XIII. Ignoring the custom of being silent before the Pope, Thérèse boldly pleaded with him to be allowed to enter Carmel before she reached the minimum required age.

The resilience of the Church was visible in the growth of mission efforts that touched the life of Thérèse directly. The context for her desire to go to the missions was France's colonial expansion to Indochina, Mexico, Tahiti, Africa, and the Crimea. Both Catholic and Protestant mission societies flourished. The Society for the Propagation of the Faith had been founded in Lyon in 1822, renewing Catholicism's outreach to the globe. In 1861 four sisters from the Lisieux Carmel made a foundation in Saigon. Thérèse's desire to go there was never fulfilled, but she lived out this dream through her correspondence with two missionaries, Adolphe Roulland and Maurice Bellière, for whom she served as spiritual director—a reversal of the gender status quo.

A second sign of the Church's inner vitality was the foundation of new religious orders such as the Marianists, the Oblates of the Immaculate Virgin Mary, the Marist Brothers, the Pallottines (whose official name was Pious Society of Missions), and the Society of Missionaries of Our Lady of Africa, known as the White Fathers. In 1830, Catherine Labouré, a Parisian Sister of Charity, had a vision of Mary that gave rise to the creation of the Miraculous Medal. The Society of St. Vincent de Paul was organized in 1833 to enlist the laity in the care of the sick and the poor. The Little Sisters of the Poor were founded in 1852.

Visible in many of the official titles of these Orders is renewed devotion to Mary. In 1854, Pius IX declared the Immaculate Conception a dogma of the Church. In 1858 Bernadette Soubirous reported eighteen appearances of the Virgin in a grotto at Lourdes. Louis-Marie Grignion de Montfort's (d. 1816) *True Devotion to Mary*, discovered in 1842, was widely read.

The spiritual strength of the Church was also visible in popular piety. Eucharistic processions, pilgrimages, parish missions, men's retreats, and youth groups attested to the vibrancy of Catholic piety. Lay Catholics were fed by Bible reading, Thomas à Kempis's *The Imitation of Christ*—written in 1420–1427 and a favorite of Thérèse's—and a book on the liturgical year.[10] Thérèse's parents modeled this type of intense lay spirituality which nurtured her own passionate spiritual journey.

Broader intellectual and cultural strains included the ongoing development of science and the new academic disciplines of psychology, sociology, and anthropology. Darwin published *Origin of Species* in 1859. In 1891, the subsequent Nobel prize-winner, Marie Curie, left her native Poland to study in Paris. Steam was harnessed to fuel manufacturing, boats, and railroads. The telephone, light, and electricity changed the way people lived as did new discoveries in how to control germs and pain (anesthesia). Nationalism flourished and wealth grew, countered by new ideas of how to organize society on the model of socialism. Leading thinkers reflected a spirit of skepticism, socialism, secularism, Deism, and atheism—all contested by the Church. Some notable names from this period include Ludwig Feuerbach (1804–1872), Karl Marx, (1818–1883), and Friedrich Nietzsche (1844–1900).

In the arts, the France of the nineteenth century produced the romanticism of Jean-Jacques Rousseau, the realism of Victor Hugo's *Les Misérables,* Balzac's *Père Goriot,* Émile Zola's *Germinal* about a mining disaster, and Gustave Falubert's *Madame Bovary.* The life of ordinary people and the hard labor of peasants and urban poor were portrayed by artists such as Renoir. We owe to the ferment and creativity of this period in France the Impressionist work of Manet and Cézanne, which would pave the way for the deconstructing cubism of Pablo Picasso. Famous composers included Claude Débussy, Charles Gounod, Gabriel Fauré, Camille Saint-Saens, and Georges Bizet. Between 1853 and 1870, Napoleon III commissioned Baron Georges Eugène Haussmann to beautify Paris with its now treasured boulevards, public parks, cafés, and the iconic Eiffel Tower, which was built as part of the 1889 World's Fair.

Strains of this world challenged the faith and seeped into Thérèse's life: her intense piety; the important role given to the Virgin Mary; a preoccupation with suffering; her awareness that priests, although called to a high calling, were "weak and fragile men" in need of prayer; and her dedication to mission. Her reason for entering Carmel, she said, was "to save souls and above all, to pray for priests."[11]

THÉRÈSE'S THEOLOGY OF THE CROSS

Thérèse's theology is both rich and elusive. As noted above, it is a wisdom theology embedded in daily life, liturgy, and spiritual practices, rather than in formal theological categories. Since she received little schooling, she depended on other sources for her theological concepts and language. These included reflection on the scriptures, *The Imitation of Christ*, the works of John of the Cross, spiritual conversations, and reading during meals. And yet, she noted that most spiritual reading gave her a headache and that Jesus had no need of books or teachers because he is the Doctor of doctors who "teaches without the noise of words."[12] Mealtime traditionally included the reading of brief biographies of deceased French Carmelites, texts that deeply influenced the way Thérèse wrote about her own death. Thus, her theology emerges out of life; her doctrine is probed through experience.

John Paul II summarized the theological topics she addressed:

> The mysteries of [Christ's] infancy, the words of his Gospel; the passion of the suffering servant engraved on his holy face, in the splendor of his glorious life, in his Eucharistic presence;... Christ's mystical body, the variety of its charisms; the gifts of the Holy Spirit; the eminent power of love...the mystery and journey of the Virgin Mary.[13]

We can also look to Thérèse for theological insight into the Church, the communion of saints, Mary, and the universal call to holiness. In addition, Thérèse had a deep sacramental consciousness that enabled her to see the closeness of God everywhere—in her family, her vocation, the Church, and nature. Her intimate experience of God's presence is revealed in an early description of a mystical moment she shared with her sister Céline (whom she called "sweet echo of my soul") in the belvedere of their elegant home in Lisieux.[14] As they discussed the saints, their eyes were drawn upward to the sky, and they felt the touch of God in the pale moon rising gently behind the trees and in the evening breeze. She compared this moment to the shared mystical experience of Augustine and his mother Monica as they looked out on their garden in a villa in Ostia, Italy.

Our interest in this chapter is Thérèse's theology of the cross—a centerpiece of her theological thought and a preoccupation of her Catholic culture. We first situate this theology of suffering within the context of nineteenth-century France. As we have noted, social upheaval, atheism, and anti-Catholic bias put the Church in the shadows and on the defensive. In response, the Church nurtured a piety that encouraged the faithful to reenact the sacrifice of the cross as a means to save the "lost" and non-believers in their midst. This included those who embraced the Revolution and the "godless" Republic, Protestants, freemasons, socialists, foreigners and Jews.

This spirituality of sacrifice provided a lens through which French Catholics could view their daily sufferings.[15] It was a way to "buy back" the wayward from perdition. Those like Thérèse, who took this piety to heart, actively desired pain, suffering, and martyrdom. French women were especially influenced by the idea of sharing in Christ's suffering. Thérèse saw herself as a member of an elite core of Catholics called to carry on Christ's redeeming work through sacrifice and martyrdom.

The cross had a pronounced, tangible presence in Thérèse's life and imagination. Mother Geneviève, the founder of the Lisieux Carmel, had placed in the convent chapel an image of the Veil of Veronica on which was imprinted the suffering face of Christ.[16] After Compline Thérèse often gathered her five novices at the granite cross in the convent courtyard to throw rose petals at the crucifix. In 1894, Thérèse painted an image of the Holy Face on a chasuble surrounded with flowers representing the members of her family. When her father died in July of 1897, his death card bore the Holy Face and above his name was written, "Lord, hide him in the secret of your Face." In August 1896, a large image of the Holy Face was placed over Thérèse's bed as she endured the final months of darkness—extreme physical pain and a searing crisis of faith. In her final moments, Thérèse looked at the crucifix and cried out: "Oh! I love Him...my God! I love You!"

We begin with Thérèse's personal experience of suffering and then examine key elements in her theology of the cross—the Holy Face, martyrdom, and joy.

Thérèse's Personal Suffering

Life brought Thérèse sustained, intense suffering and loss. In a letter to her sister Marie, Thérèse wrote: "He [Jesus] has found us worthy to pass through the crucible of suffering."[17] She believed that her call to be the spouse of Christ meant that she was destined to suffer from her "very infancy."[18] On her death bed, Thérèse told Mother Agnes of her lifelong desire to suffer. She remembered that at her first Communion, she had begged Jesus to change all earthly consolations into bitterness. She had suffered the devastating loss of her mother when she was only four years old, and she lost her father in 1894 after a severe mental illness. At age ten, Thérèse suffered an acute illness that lasted about two months and included body spasms, paranoia, hallucinations, screaming, and moments of terror. In addition to the stress of difficulties at school and the departure of Pauline for Carmel, it is possible that Thérèse had become infected with the tuberculosis virus that went to her brain, only later to go into remission until near the end of her life.[19] Of Pauline's departure, Thérèse wrote:

> I understood I was about to lose my second Mother!...in one
> instant I understood what life was; until then I had never seen

it so bad; but it appeared to me in all its reality, and I saw it was nothing but continual suffering and separation.... I said in the depths of my heart; "Pauline is lost to me!"[20]

Then, her sister Marie, her "other mother," left for Carmel. On her own entry into Carmel Thérèse wrote: "Suffering opened wide its arms to me and I threw myself into them with love."[21] During her time at Carmel, she experienced the devastating illness of her father, intense spiritual aridity, physical discomfort from the convent diet and cold, and a painful death from tuberculosis. In addition to the physical suffering from these illnesses, mental dysfunction and tuberculosis also carried a stigma of shame—suggesting moral weakness—an especially poignant trial for a family whose life revolved around practicing virtue.

Thérèse faced this suffering by transforming it into a way of the cross. Her eventual thirst for suffering led her to see it as the only desirable thing in her life, a precious gift from God, a form of heaven on earth. For Thérèse, humans were superior to angels because of their capacity to suffer. She saw her vocation as winning souls for God, a feat that was accomplished through participation in the cross. We know Thérèse aimed some of the fruits of her redemptive suffering at priests who did not live up to their vocations.[22] She said her reason for entering Carmel was "to save souls and above all, to pray for priests."[23]

THE HOLY FACE

A particular and distinctive embodiment of Thérèse's theology of the cross was her focus on the face of Jesus—an image familiar to Thérèse from childhood and linked to the cloth with which Veronica was said to have wiped Jesus's face on the way to Calvary.[24] Thérèse's official name in religion was St. Thérèse of the Child Jesus and the Holy Face.

The spiritual theology linked to the first part of her name is familiar to anyone who has heard or read about her Little Way. Like the child Jesus, Thérèse advocated a spirituality of childlike trust.[25] She was a "poster child" for Jesus's call to allow the little ones to come to him

(Luke 18:16; Matthew 19:14). Less attention is paid to the second part of her name—the Holy Face—a name she chose when she received the veil at Carmel on January 10, 1889. As a child, Thérèse belonged to the Atoning Confraternity of the Holy Face of Tours. At Carmel, she heard about this popular French devotion from Sr. Agnès during their father's illness. It can be traced back to 1845 when Sr. Marie de Saint-Pierre (1816–1848), a Carmelite nun at Tours, consecrated herself to the Holy Face to make reparation for the offenses against God in what was seen as a godless, secular time. Thérèse mentioned the "Holy Face" often in her writings, but she discarded the theological idea of reparation in favor of merciful love. After Easter of 1896 when she entered into the suffering of the cross in an acute fashion, she no longer mentions the Holy Face— perhaps living it made speaking about it less meaningful.

In August of 1896, on the feast of the Transfiguration, Thérèse and two novices made a formal consecration to the Holy Face.[26] In it, they speak of love—wanting to dry the gentle face of Jesus who speaks to them as the Lover of the Song of Songs: "Open to me my sisters, my beloved brides, for *my Face* is covered with dew and *my hair* with the drops of the night."[27] We know that Thérèse wore on her chest a small pouch with some medals and prayers in it, including a photo and lock of hair belonging to Sr. Marie de Saint-Pierre, and an image of the Holy Face of Tours, under which was written her shortest prayer: "Make me resemble you, Jesus!" Thérèse's sister Céline wrote:

> Devotion to the Holy Face was, for Thérèse, the crown and complement of her love for the Sacred Humanity of Our Lord. This Sacred Face was the mirror wherein she beheld the Heart and Soul of her Well-Beloved. Just as the picture of a loved one serves to bring the whole person before us, so in the Holy Face of Christ, Thérèse beheld the entire Humanity of Jesus. We can say unequivocally that this devotion was the burning inspiration of the Saint's life…. All her writings—the Autobiography,

the Letters and the Poems—are impregnated with the love of this same Adorable Face.[28]

Céline may have been especially attuned to this aspect of Thérèse's thought. Céline had been trained as a painter, later turning to photography. She brought to Carmel the camera she used to take most of the pictures of Thérèse that we possess, some of which were highly edited. After Thérèse's death, Céline oversaw the production and dissemination of these images.[29]

Much of Thérèse's image of the Holy Face as hidden and rejected came from Isaiah:

> He had no form or majesty that we should look at him; nothing in his appearance that we should desire him. He was despised and rejected by others; a man of suffering and acquainted with infirmity; and as one from whom others hide their faces; he was despised, and we held him of no account. (53:2–3)

Shortly before her death, Thérèse commented to Pauline:

> The words in Isaiah: "No stateliness here, no majesty, no beauty, as we gaze upon him, to win our hearts. Nay, here is one despised, left out of all human reckoning; bowed with misery, and no stranger to weakness; how should we recognize that face? How should we take any account of him, a man so despised"—these words were the basis of my whole worship of the Holy Face.... I, too wanted to be without comeliness and beauty, alone to tread the grapes, unknown to all creatures.[30]

Thérèse placed the face of the suffering Lord at the center of her spiritual life. "Her whole life in Christ is concentrated into her devotion to the Holy Face."[31]

Thérèse called this face her "heritage, the coin given to her to redeem souls, her native land, her kingdom of love where she resolved to live unknown and alone."[32] Thus, the "face" in Thérèse's name refers to the face of Christ's suffering love as well as to her own face that she desired to be shaped in imitation of Christ. Christ's cry on the cross—"My God, my God, why have you forsaken me?"—became her own.

In April of 1889, Thérèse wrote to Céline: "The music of our suffering, united to His Passion, ravishes His Heart.... See His adorable face; notice how the Eyes are veiled and lowered; study His wounds. Fix your eyes upon His Countenance...[to] see how He loves us."[33] In another letter to Celine written later that year, Thérèse wrote of Jesus, "He wants only a *look, a sigh,* but a look and a sigh that are for *Him alone*!"[34] Thomas Nevin describes the two parts of Thérèse's name as "the alpha and omega of her Christology: the Incarnation and the Crucifixion; the swaddling clothes and the shroud; the humbling of God to helpless infancy and the redemptive Passion."[35] For Thérèse, childhood trust and suffering were two aspects of the same reality. But Mother Agnès (her sister Pauline) would testify that Thérèse's devotion to the Child Jesus could not be compared to her devotion to the Holy Face.

Thérèse experienced Jesus as someone who faced her in a selfless way. Those who faced Jesus physically during his lifetime and those who faced him in spiritual ways throughout history were changed by the encounter. The Gospels portray Jesus primarily in his face-to-face relationships with others—welcoming, non-judgmental, accepting. In Jesus we have a divine face that is shockingly, scandalously hospitable to all. "Facing" is one way to think about the meaning of salvation, a many-faceted transformation that happens in our relationship with God and the world.[36]

But at the end of the Jesus story we are left with a dead face, which Thérèse mines for its theological implications. It is remarkable but culturally understandable that it took Christian art almost nine hundred years to portray Jesus as dead on the cross. The first images were of a face that was alive with open eyes. In the Hebrew Scriptures the word *panim* is translated as "face, presence, sight, countenance, person." Adam and Eve hid themselves from the *panim* of the Lord. The term also shows up in the story of Jacob wrestling at Jabbok (Genesis 32), the giving of the

Torah on Mount Sinai, and in the suffering servant of Isaiah. Sin and its consequences are registered in bodies and especially on faces.

Thérèse's life exemplifies the Christian mystery of death-into-life brought about by transforming love. In her generous love for others, for missionaries, and for the Church, Thérèse suffered but she never severed her pain from the joy of God's resurrected love. By linking her life with the crucified love of Christ, she avoided the kind of superficial, "perfect" relationships that remain flawlessly mutual, open, rewarding, and peaceful.

If the face of Jesus on the cross is intrinsic to salvation, it can't simply signify a radical rupture and loss (experienced firsthand by John, Mary Magdalene, and the other disciples). It must also be the face that brings life to all creation. Because Christ died for us, the cross calls us to responsibility. The resurrection reveals and empowers our vocation to forgive and be forgiven freely; to live in Spirit-filled responsibility; and to call others to this "way." As Thérèse knew well, the theology of the face is the key to this power.

Martyrdom

Thérèse spoke of her vocation to be Carmelite, Spouse, and Mother. But she adds Warrior, Priest, Apostle, Doctor, Crusader, Papal Guard— male roles that were beyond her reach as a woman. Martyrdom has been a gender-equalizer from the very earliest days of Christianity—Perpetua and Felicitas (martyred in North Africa in 203) are familiar names from the Roman Catholic liturgy.

Thérèse expressed a desire "to die on the field of battle in defense of the Church."[37] The call to martyrdom was the dream of her youth that grew within Carmel's cloisters. The vocabulary of martyrdom showed up early in her life. This precocious, tearful teenager described the three days she had to wait for her Uncle Isidore's decision about entering Carmel as a "terrible martyrdom" and compared it to Jesus's agony in the garden. She tells us that she was not happy with only one kind of martyrdom. She wanted all types.[38] On a holy card imprinted with an image of the crucified, Thérèse wrote that the moan that escaped from the heart of Jesus on the cross was impressed on her heart.

One of the martyrdoms that drew Thérèse was that of the missionary. But the trajectory of Thérèse's life soon revealed that she was not destined to become a martyr in the literal sense of the term. The space in which she lived out this call was physically very small—the four walls of Carmel. This meant that her self-denial and sacrifice were severely limited to the daily annoyances and challenges of living in close quarters with a small group of women, some of whom were her blood sisters, while others, less attractive to her, challenged her to her depths. Her way of the cross meant suffering injustice in silence: guarding her tongue, serving without recognition, seeking out the most irritating members of the community, accepting the faults of others, refusing to impose her will on others. Thus this Little Way was also a Big Way in its patience, fidelity, and sacrifice of ego—always a significant challenge of the spiritual life.

The use of military imagery to describe the spiritual life is common throughout the tradition and was especially prominent in nineteenth-century France. Thérèse associated military imagery with Joan of Arc, whom she admired like an elder sister who had suffered nobly. From passages on Joan of Arc that Thérèse recorded as composition exercises at school to the numerous poems, hymns, and plays she wrote about Joan (in which she played Joan), Thérèse was captivated by a desire to imitate her great deeds.[39] Thérèse must have been disappointed when she realized that she would not die on the field of battle or at the stake. She spoke of her vocation to martyrdom not as helping get the King of France crowned, but as getting the King of Heaven loved. She wrote: "My mission will be accomplished according to God's will, like Joan of Arc's, in spite of the envy of men." Her sword would be love.

THE PARADOX: JOY IN SUFFERING

In his review of the 1987 film *Thérèse*, the late Roger Ebert commented that "the movie is one long question: What was the secret of Thérèse Martin's joy...why was she so happy?" We have noted that Thérèse's joy began in her family where she was surrounded by love and affirmation. But she admits that her early joy was grounded in her good works, and only much later does she discover genuine joy in the cross.

Inspired in part by the spirit of Francis of Assisi, Thérèse eventually discovered that love brought true joy in suffering. This provocative and paradoxical theological stance is based on her deeply personal relationship with Christ—one that allowed Thérèse to see only love and tenderness in the suffering face of Jesus—a love that produces joy. Five hundred years earlier, Julian of Norwich recorded her transformation in love and joy through meditation on the face of the crucified. These holy, theologically astute women invite us to enter into the mystery of the Holy Face and discover who God is and who we are in the face of a love that knows no bounds.

Thérèse is very deliberate about choosing to see the glass half full. "I always see the good side of things.... If I have nothing but pure suffering, if the heavens are so black that I see no break in the clouds, well, I make this my joy!"[40] Underneath her simple language we sense a will of steel. Her will also extended to her body in her choice to smile constantly and reflect a peaceful demeanor—even in the midst of excruciating suffering (Matthew 6:16–18). She would not have known the science that tells us bodily behaviors can affect inner dispositions and she challenges the hegemony of psychology's admonition to express true feelings in the interest of mental health.

Thérèse's theological creativity is visible in her desire to give God joy and consolation. She experiences Jesus smiling at her when she sighs and describes heaven as "his ravishing Smile,"[41] but she also reciprocates: "I want no other joy than that of making you smile";[42] "I want to overwhelm you with caresses."[43]

In a letter to Celine, she wrote: "Let us make our life a continual sacrifice, a martyrdom of love, in order to console Jesus."[44] In her letters, Thérèse mentions nineteen times her desire to console Jesus.[45] In Thérèse's second play on Joan of Arc, the archangel Gabriel encourages the imprisoned maid with the words: "Joan, your name has consoled Jesus!"

The paradox of joy in suffering deepens in Thérèse's teaching that she is called to suffer without joy or courage or strength. "What an unspeakable joy to carry our Crosses FEEBLY."[46] Her model is Jesus who, she says, "suffered in sadness!" She adds an astute psychological note: "Without sadness would the soul suffer!"[47]

But at the end after a painful cauterizing treatment for her tuberculosis, she said: "I am as one risen…don't be troubled about me, for I have come to a point where I cannot suffer any longer, because all suffering is sweet to me."[48]

Often ideas about divine perfection make it almost impossible for us to imagine that God might need us. But when theology is grounded in the human experience of a love affair with God, it makes perfect sense to imagine God as wanting and needing our love. Because Thérèse was especially sensitive to Jesus's need for joy when he suffered on the cross, she assumed the responsibility to offer joy to him through her own joy in suffering. We witness here a deeply mutual relationship—a commonplace in the mystical tradition. In the poem "My Heaven on Earth!..." she writes:

> Jesus, your ineffable image
> Is the star that guides my steps.
> Ah! you know, your sweet Face
> Is for me Heaven on earth.
> My love discovers the charms
> Of your Face adorned with tears.
> I smile through my own tears
> When I contemplate your sorrows….
> …
> Your Face is my only Homeland.
> It's my Kingdom of love,
> It's my cheerful Meadow,
> Each day, my sweet Sun.
> …
> It's my Rest, my Sweetness

And my melodious Lyre....
Your Face, O my sweet Savior,
Is the Divine bouquet of Myrrh
I want to keep on my heart...[49]

Thérèse was fond of images of Jesus in his vulnerability—as a baby, asleep in the boat during a storm—she assured him that she would let him rest—and on the cross. She teaches the valuable insight that at the center of salvation is a God who is helpless in face of his love for humanity.[50]

Thérèse expressed gratitude for this vocation to joyful suffering. It was hard won. She wrote: "I thank you, O my God! for all the graces you have granted me, especially the grace of making me pass through the crucible of suffering. It is with joy I shall contemplate You to the last day carrying the scepter of your Cross. Since you deigned to give me a share in this very precious Cross, I hope in Heaven to resemble you and to see shining in my glorified body the sacred stigmata of Your Passion."[51] Thérèse even spoke of using sacrifices and joys to take Jesus captive, making him a prisoner by offering him the joys he scatters in our path to charm our hearts.

But in the end, Thérèse did not know the final consolation of the blessed. In the end, she remained in darkness, living only by faith. During the final eighteen months of her life, Thérèse had become a different person. From the child who kept count of her sacrifices and dreamt of a divine reward, she became an adult with insight into atheism and despair. In the midst of her agony she says: "I'm very happy, but I can't say that I [am] experiencing a living joy and transports of happiness, no!"[52] There is heroism in Thérèse's fidelity to God and her willingness to trust even in the midst of total darkness. Within and without, she is in excruciating pain. Her joy is beneath, in the depths of her soul.

She expresses this joy in a poem titled "My Joy!" written in January of 1897, the year of her death.

Joy is in my heart.
This joy is not ephemeral.
I possess it forever.
Like the springtime rose,
It smiles at me every day.
…
My joy is to love suffering.
…
My joy is the Holy Will
Of Jesus, my only love,
So I live without any fear.[53]

Thérèse's Theology Today

What are we to make of Thérèse's theology of the cross in a culture that demands instant gratification and comfort, flees suffering, and spends billions on "self-care"? The theology and spirituality of nineteenth-century France seem far removed indeed. The cultural trappings that allowed her to make theological sense of her life no longer exist. Nor is it wise to put her on a pedestal with no hard questions asked. Few of us resonate with Thérèse's sense of being separated forever "from that world which you have cursed."[54] Thérèse's family life appears opaque and unreal when compared with today's youth with their cell phones, sports, the Web, skateboards, makeup, and stores full of clothes, gadgets, and distractions. What would Thérèse think of the mantra that liturgy is "boring"; of our religiously pluralistic, global, democratic culture; of liberation theology with its distinctive approach to the cross?

Every era must come to terms with the cross through its own distinctive theology and practices.[55] We admire Thérèse for her courage to embrace the cross and make it an anchor of her theology. She viewed all the basic truths of Christian theology through the lens of the Holy Face. She was able to do this because, in the final analysis, she saw in the face of the Crucified only an immeasurably tender love. But aspects of the perception and pursuit of suffering in late nineteenth-century French Roman

Catholic spirituality are mischievous if they lead to loveless practices that disdain or destroy the body; nurture a sense of victimization; dehumanize women; or lead to self-preoccupation and self-congratulation.

Our understanding of salvation history has also grown and changed. We no longer focus on "saving souls." The mid-twentieth-century Roman Catholic practice of "ransoming" pagan babies" seems bizarre only half a century later. But we can adapt Thérèse's ways of loving the neighbor to our own situation, inspired by her to put the well-being of others before our own. Does our growth in compassion fuel our desire for dignity and holiness for every human? We are also more likely to embrace a Christology in which the cross is closely knit to Christ's entire life and resurrection. We may not think so much in terms of God's "sending" suffering, or see suffering as an automatic sign of divine friendship, or a way to attain a higher place in heaven. And our ability to inflict horrendous destruction on others through slavery and torture reminds us that not all suffering makes us better people. We are less likely to think that God needs our suffering and more prone to focus on God's demand of love, which almost always involves suffering.

But Thérèse is a master at communicating the realness of the God-man with whom she risked all by entering into an all-or-nothing love relationship.[56] She shows us an infinite love that harmonizes well with our modern penchant to view the Holy Face in historical, fleshly terms. Our theology may emphasize more the positive effects of this love on the world, but Thérèse provides an important perspective in her kenotic, emptying, hidden Christ. We may emphasize more the joys of everyday life as genuine revelation of God, but Thérèse plants the seed of desire to abandon ourselves to a loving God in all parts of our lives.

But having Thérèse named a Doctor of the Universal Church is certainly not to engage in a slavish imitation of her theology and life. The cultural trappings that allowed her to make sense of her life no longer exist. We are reminded that every Christian is unique just as every saint and Doctor of the Church is unique. One pattern never fits all. Few Christians are called to an enclosed contemplative life. The more common setting for the imitation of Christ is the complex busy world—work, children, sex, and taxes. In all these holy places we participate in and extend the suffering and joy embodied in the historical Jesus. Monastic theology and spirituality led Thérèse to say that she found joy only in God and not in creatures, even though her life too was focused on the love of others. But all creatures, all of nature, and all of culture are blessed and imbued with divine love and grace. Sin, not the world, is the enemy.

Thérèse beckons all Christians to the Little Way, a way in which even the smallest sacrifice is important. She did not allow

> one little sacrifice to escape, not one look, one word, profiting by all the smallest things and doing them through love. I desire to suffer for love and even to rejoice through love…. While I am strewing my flowers, I shall sing, for could one cry while doing such a joyous action? I shall sing even when I must gather my flowers in the midst of thorns, and my song will be all the more melodious in proportion to the length and sharpness of the thorns.[57]

Thérèse's understanding of suffering was not static, nor should ours be. It grew and changed over the course of her short life. At the outset, she saw suffering and sacrifice as ways to earn merit to redeem sinners and earn a high place in heaven. But over time, especially in the final eighteen months of her life, she discovered a God who was not at all interested in appeasement but only in lavish love. Her insight into love grew from an embrace of personal virtue and sacrifice as a way to garner heavenly reward—with the inherent temptation to arrogance—to an outward gaze toward the "other" and a surrender that mirrored the ignominious death of Jesus. She allowed God to transform the bitter tears of her early life into joy. Fear became desire. Dread became delight. Consolation followed embrace of her vocation to the cross. Human resignation and struggle in the face of loss were transformed. She voiced a paradox of the mystical way: "My joy," she said, "consists in being deprived of all joy here on earth."[58] Amazingly, she ended up in a place that was quite different from her upbringing and her culture.

In ending her life in excruciating aridity, pain, and doubt, Thérèse mirrors the Crucified, providing a model especially for those who are tempted to give up hope—the poor, prisoners, refugees, the elderly, and all who are seriously ill. Thérèse could not have foreseen that she would provide companionship and insight for many in the twentieth century who experienced excruciating suffering and abandonment in trenches and death camps.[59] Her discovery that in her own eyes, she was unable to "suffer generously and nobly" invites us to view our own weakness and failure as an invitation to throw ourselves into the open arms of God's mercy.[60]

But we need to adjust some of Thérèse's emphases. Along with the idea of the Little Way, most Christians view the Holy Face in historical, fleshly terms. It says something concrete, earthly and positive about God—it is the divine in human form. Thérèse's kenotic, emptying, hidden Christ is part of the theological picture, but not the whole. Over the course of a lifetime, Christians may find that Christ speaks most powerfully in joy, while at other times, it is in moments of crisis and loss. Most of us meet God in the small and large joys of daily life as well as in its trials. Thérèse helps us with the latter more than with the former. Her universal message beckons us to notice and turn to God's love in all of life in an effort to live always in harmony with God's eternal loving thirst for the world.

The theology of Thérèse of the Child Jesus and the Holy Face extends the example of Mary and the Magdalene, as well as the medieval theologies of Bonaventure and Julian of Norwich, challenging Christians to spend time "facing" and "being faced" at the cross. The prayerful, attentive practice of facing the cross can open new doors of insight for us just as it did for Thérèse. Theologies of the cross draw us into the shattering, yet hope-filled truth of incarnation and freeing love. They also inevitably take us out of ourselves to the world near and far. "Facing" the Crucified can reveal layers of self-identity, bringing home to us the truth that we, and every created thing, are made in God's image and loved wildly by this God on the cross. Thérèse wrote: "Just one glance of yours makes my beatitude."[61] Thérèse's way echoes Paul's wisdom: "And all of us, with unveiled faces, seeing the glory of the Lord as though reflected in a mirror, are being transformed into the same image from one degree of glory to another; for this comes from the Lord, the Spirit" (2 Corinthians 3:18).

Contemplation of a face is a complex process in which we attend, notice, and love the other in a spirit of openness and curiosity. It takes a lifetime to learn to face others in this way—even when we have mentors like Thérèse who had a practiced eye that could discern the difference between true and false sight. This process can be an individual exercise, but ultimately, the work must be done together in diverse, inclusive communities of faith. Contemplation of the Holy Face might include a prayer of petition for the grace to face each other as gift—encouraging, prodding, and challenging each other to find twenty-first-century ways to live out the truth discovered in the face of the crucified.

Thérèse's experience of suffering and her love of the cross led her to fashion and express theological insight. A universal strain in Thérèse's theology of the cross is the presence of grace. In the face of God's eternally magnanimous love and mercy, we fall appallingly short. But it doesn't matter. Thérèse portrays a God who unfailingly invites us to trust and love, and her theology of the cross calls us back to this precious truth. With Mary Magdalene and the prodigal son, the woman caught in adultery, and the woman of Samaria—Thérèse calls all to absorb, echo, and live her words: "No one could frighten me, for I know what to think of his mercy and love."

Theological Reflection

- Describe an experience of being face-to-face with someone important in your life. How so you link this "facing" to God, Christ, the Holy Spirit?

- Spend ten minutes before a crucifix, gazing into the face of Christ. What happens? Who are you in this moment? To what virtues does the experience call you?
- Recall a moment in which you felt extreme desolation. How did you deal with this? How might Thérèse help you face this suffering with patience and love?
- How might Thérèse shed light on moments of doubt and questions about faith? Listen to Gabriel's Fauré's *Requiem* (1888) which has been described as a musical complement to Thérèse's theology: no fire and brimstone drama; assurance of heaven as a place of happiness; gentleness overcoming fear.
- What is your reaction to Thérèse's phrase "the music of our suffering"?

CHAPTER SIX

Women's Theological Voices
Retrieval and Renewal

We began this journey through the theologies of the four women Doctors of the Church with a discussion about the various types of theology—academic, imaginative, vernacular, mystical. We noted that none of the four women who have been declared Doctors of the Church in the Roman Catholic Church fit neatly into what we normally think of when we think of theology—a more formal, academic genre. But in their texts, the visage of teacher shines through unmistakably.

Like Anselm, Aquinas, and Bonaventure, their aim is to instruct in doctrine and holiness of life. They are motivated by the desire to share with others the theological insights they have received from God through their own experience and openness to grace. They are good teachers inasmuch as they communicate with confidence, convincing readers that their theology is true, worthy of consideration, and integrated with everyday life. In naming them Doctors of the Church, the universal Church agrees. Next steps involve reading and reflecting on their own words—many excellent translations of these primary texts are easily accessible.

It is appropriate for the Church to identify authoritative figures who illuminate in reliable ways the theological heritage of the Church—Bible, Trinity, Jesus Christ, Holy Spirit, Christian anthropology, sin, salvation, eschatology, ethics, the Church, and the People of God. They bring to life the doctrine of the communion of saints, sharing their charism of teaching with the wider body of Christ (1 Corinthians 12). These women, acknowledged by the Church, do not represent an exhaustive or perfect account of Christian theology, but they are authentic voices, echoing the voice of the ultimate, divine Teacher.

This theological work is important because "the written tradition of Christian theology has been constituted by the exclusion of women" (and others).[1] It is amazing that any woman found ways to enter the theological tradition. The judgment that women are inferior human beings and particularly stunted in their intelligence has dogged women down the centuries. Even worse, this damning judgment has been internalized, blocking, contorting, and silencing women's voices. "It is impossible not to grieve over the holocaust of women's wisdom that is part of the collateral damage of Christianity."[2]

Nevertheless, for some women, writing has been a source of liberation. It has produced confidence in the Tradition and authority in the Spirit, and called established authority into question. It has brought legitimate power and well-being to women authors and salvific wisdom to the Christian community. By turning to their experience as women; employing styles and genres not typically considered theological; and reshaping older genres, women have opened the windows of theology, Scripture, liturgy, and spirituality to allow fresh air and new ideas to enter. They brought poetry, imagery, music, prophecy, and passionate feeling to the task, along with reason and logic. By creating a new theological language out of their experience as women, they changed what counts as theology and who counts as theologians. They call women to temper the nay-saying voices in their heads; honor the gift of wisdom that is theirs; and create spaces in which female theological voices are welcome. Theologian Wendy Farley writes: "theology is not primarily texts but a kind of desire that employs thought as a religious practice. I feel grateful to the women who have been writing for thousands of years, creating and preserving theological wisdom while remaining almost completely invisible."[3]

It is inevitable that through the ages, the Church experiences periods in which its theology and doctrine become moribund. Hearing the same words and ideas over and over again can deaden what was once a thoroughly life-transforming experience. Theology stays alive by being in dialogue with the present moment. Academic theologians rightly build on what has gone before, a process which is integral to a faith that values tradition. The challenge is to remember that behind the words is a love affair with God. The old words invite us to begin or deepen our own relationships with the divine and in turn, find the images, the concepts, the language to express our contemporary experience of revelation.

Without formal theological education, these four women relied heavily on the promptings of the Holy Spirit, their innate intelligence, and their individual and communal experience. We might say that their theologies are close to the ground. They created theological syntheses that are strikingly different from Thomas Aquinas's *Summa Theologiae*, but their work provides an important addition and counterpoint to other types of theology. Since the theologies of these women emerge more directly out of their daily living and activity in the world and cloister, their theologies are rightly called wisdom theologies. They integrate the theoretical and the practical; intellectual acumen and passion; head with heart. The outcome of this more existential, mystical, imaginative theology is to wake us up so that we allow their poetry, imagery, and prophecy to enliven our theology and our Christian lives.

There are aspects of any theology that made eminent sense in the original context, but don't easily translate into our own. And yet, the popularity of women saints and mystics among wide segments of society attests to contemporary hunger for transcendent meaning, and to the fact that they indeed have something to offer. They strike a chord with women and men of the twenty-first century who are seeking more creative and more engaged approaches to Christian discipleship.

As we work to recover this female theological heritage, we need to be alert to elements that might be harmful, and committed to interpreting the texts in light of "the signs of our times": the communication revolution; the possibility of a nuclear holocaust; ecological degradation; global economics; the discoveries of science; interfaith dialogue; and a Church whose outlook and image has changed dramatically. Our emphasis on class, race, gender, and sexual orientation would be foreign indeed in centuries past. We need to take account of these issues in our theologies today. But before we summarize how these theologies continue to speak to us in life-giving ways, we need to address some of the challenges involved in discerning what should not be brought forward.

CRITICAL REFLECTION

I suspect that Hildegard, Catherine, Teresa, and Thérèse would cringe at the thought of being placed on pedestals, removed from the nitty-gritty of real life. They all both transcend and are bound by their personalities, geography, life experience, and the socio-religious currents of their time. It is true that all human beings share experiences of war, illness, sin, death, joy, gratitude, and praise. However, the details and the meaning of each experience are forever embedded in historically particular circumstances. Christians in every age seek to know and love God, but, in each setting, this means different things, generating different ideas and practices.

In their independence and creativity of thought, these women challenge us to read carefully, reflect deeply and then make our own decisions about what they say. When we ask of what use this work is to us we need to do so intelligently. A simplistic, naïve retrieval would surely not do justice to the work of these four illustrious women. Honoring their memory requires effort—study, serious reflection, and analysis. They want us to commit to discovering the truth just as they did.

The following select group of examples may sharpen our vision toward an honest, realistic, historically conscious appropriation of this material. I begin with issues that are likely to cause problems for twenty-first-century readers and then address elements from this material that might be retrieved to our benefit.

SUFFERING

As we have seen, Catherine, Teresa, Thérèse, and Hildegard endured many kinds of suffering in the courses of their lives.[4] All suffered from illnesses—some brought on by natural causes, some the result of severe ascetic practices that damaged their bodies. (Hildegard is an exception, for while she experienced migraine headaches since childhood, her life was governed by a Benedictine Rule of moderation.) All suffered from outside criticism, due in large measure to their choice to break rules and customs. In a variety of ways, they pushed the boundaries for acceptable female behavior in their time. Their courageous lifestyles inevitably induced a degree of self-doubt, another grievous form of suffering.

Each of these women Doctors of the Church was influenced by the various theologies of suffering prominent in her day, which may or may not fit our time. For example, we no longer view suffering as a consequence of sin, a problematic interpretation of the story of the Fall in Genesis. Catherine, Teresa, and Thérèse chose to mortify their bodies in ways that are unimaginable and rightly repugnant to twenty-first-century Christians. It is not that modern Christians are wimps—it is rather the case that practices such as extreme fasting or self-flagellation are no longer seen as meaningful ways for the community to engage with the suffering Christ. Any choice to fast today must also take into consideration the scourges of bulimia and anorexia.

But Carmelite sister Constance Fitzgerald cautions against throwing the baby out with the bathwater. For example, she invites us to learn from the way Thérèse's intense movement toward suffering was a response to extravagant love. She wonders whether the contemporary impulse to flee suffering at all cost, or even "our necessary and healthy turning away" from it might result in a loss of passion and depth.[5]

The alluring invitation of the material we have examined is to delve deeply into the relationship of love and suffering. What does it mean for us to be disciples of Jesus Christ in the ways he lived, died and rose from the dead? How do we experience love and suffering in our families, friendships, Church, and workplace? Is it possible to love without suffering? Answers to these questions vary depending on one's lifestyle. Living in a monastic setting involves a certain amount of "Lent" in the form of vows, a Rule and ascetic practices that are chosen and regulated. The lives of busy laypeople play out on a different stage. "Lent" might include the challenges of family relationships; social violence, addiction; and the economic insecurity of workers, refugees, and the military.

But in spite of these differences, these Doctors of the Church witness to the discovery of joy within suffering. They grew into the truth that love makes for "light burdens" (Matthew 11:30) and hope. Early in her *Dialogue,* Catherine offers a word of hope to a corrupt and struggling Church. God says,

I tell you further: the more the mystic body of holy Church is filled with troubles now, the more it will abound in delight and consolation…. So be glad in your bitterness. For I, eternal Truth, promise to refresh you, and after your bitterness I will give you consolation, along with great suffering, in the reform of holy Church.[6]

Even the extreme sin of the Church does not have the power to win out over the promise of joy and consolation made by eternal Truth.

We can all point to an experience in life that proves unequivocally that love makes suffering a joy. A natural, spontaneous response to suffering is to complain and/or wish it would go away. And in certain settings, this is indeed what is called for. But Catherine, Teresa, Thérèse, and Hildegard offer spiritual meanings worthy of our consideration. While we must be wary of the particular ascetic ways they embraced, they provide theological insight about the Christian calling to walk with Jesus to the cross; to develop ever deeper compassion for all who suffer; to do all in our power to alleviate suffering in concrete and creative action; to find meaning in our own suffering; and to allow love to work in us so that our suffering is endured, if not welcomed, with generosity and joy.

Dualism

Our penchant for dualism, in which the body, sex, money, or "the world" is seen as an obstacle to the spiritual journey, dies hard. This viewpoint includes the subtle ways women are judged less holy, beautiful, powerful, or intelligent than men. In amazing ways for their times, these women managed to escape aspects of a non-incarnational theology. Nevertheless, the air they breathed was suffused with dualistic ideas.

Hildegard, Catherine, Teresa, and Thérèse were aware of God's presence in nature, but they could have had no inkling of our call to reverse the planetary destruction we face today. The doctrines of creation and incarnation demand that we see the holiness of all matter. We also struggle to bless our bodies and sexuality as gifts of God in ways that were not possible in the context of medieval monastic life. Dualism prevents us from seeing that marriage, work in the world, money, politics, and education, are primary sources for theology. *In and of themselves,* they constitute the way of holiness.

While the texts we have studied are steeped in the dualisms of the Tradition, they also escape them, inviting us to interpret the doctrines of creation, incarnation, grace, and Holy Spirit in new ways. How do we understand the theology of the refrain in Genesis: "and it was good" (Genesis 1:31)? It is no longer theologically legitimate to rate soul over body; intellect over emotion; head over heart; Church over world; prayer over works; interior over exterior. All of history—culture, politics, economics, business, the arts, our bodies, sexuality, nature—is made irrevocably good. The divine presence haunts every atom.

Atonement Theology

The question about the "why" of Jesus's life, death, and resurrection has occupied theologians since the writing of the New Testament. The names we assign to why Jesus became human include "redemption" or "salvation." In different historical periods, theologians have used a variety of tools to name this experience of death transformed into life. The feudal concept that the sin of humanity required reparation to God by a divine peer emerged in the twelfth century and was most enduringly articulated by Anselm of Canterbury. This idea of atonement has had a long run. All the authors we have studied were influenced by this feudal metaphor.

For example, Catherine's theology of atonement may make her a loyal daughter of Anselm, but it creates obstacles for contemporary readers. She writes in *The Dialogue:*

> So to undo the corruption and death of humankind and to bring you back to the grace you had lost through sin, I, exaltedness, united myself with the baseness of your humanity. For my divine justice demanded suffering in atonement for sin. But I cannot suffer. And you, being only human, cannot make adequate atonement.... But for this sin you could not make

full atonement either for yourself or for others since it was committed against me, and I am infinite Goodness.[7]

If we understand the theological world in which Catherine lived, we can read about "divine justice demanding suffering in atonement for sin" as just one way to think about salvation—and one we are not likely to embrace.

This does not mean that we need to dismiss Catherine's theology as useless to us. At times, she escapes the reigning theology, inserting an alternate idea in which it is desire that redeems.[8] In addition, Catherine's language about blood might provoke us to reflect on what blood means to us, who sheds blood and why, and how we might relate it to love as she does. We can let her have her viewpoint and also search for a theology of salvation with different emphases. We may be drawn to other metaphors that focus on God's infinite love or Christ's friendship. We imagine Christ as a Jewish man who lived a life with and for others. His choices and commitments, his willingness to stand up for the poor, and his commitment to renewal, resulted in a bloody death. His life of love brought about redemption, new life, and new ways to love.

A corollary of atonement theology involves the idea of merit. Christians were encouraged to make sacrifices to redeem sinners or to attain a higher place in heaven. In the background of atonement theology is a God angry at the ingratitude of humanity, and demanding satisfaction. When we encounter atonement theology from past centuries, it appears puzzling and unhelpful. We have to translate this framework into other, more meaningful terms. For example, another explanation of the cross is that it was the inevitable outcome of Jesus's life of love, compassion, and the courage to confront pride, apathy, and the misuse of power. His story is mirrored in the lives of prophets from Isaiah to John the Baptist to Dietrich Bonhoeffer and Martin Luther King.

WISDOM FOR OUR TIMES

Each person who absorbs the theologies of these four women Doctors of the Church will find a range of insights that support and enrich contemporary theology and spirituality.

From this very long list, I have chosen six themes that seem particularly relevant to our twenty-first-century world.

A Broader Understanding of Theology

Part of the valuable legacy of these four women Doctors of the Church is how they have led the Church to a broader understanding of what theology is and how it functions. To limit theology to the formal, schematized expression of the academy is to miss out on its existential dimensions and the rich metaphoric, image-laden language these women employed.

This theology relies heavily on Scripture and the liturgy—two of theology's most important sources. These women were exposed daily to biblical texts, liturgical prayer, and sermons, as well as personal prayer that resulted in a deep appropriation of this material. Often they memorized or recorded passages, making them integral to their own thought processes which overflowed into their theologies. Hildegard, Catherine, and Teresa had access to libraries and to conversations with learned monks and priests. The women lead us to our own prayerful reading of the Bible. The high level of education in many parts of the world also makes it possible for lay Christians to read secondary literature that enriches by its sheer variety of theological approaches.

An Invitation to Become Theologians

Happily we live in a time in which large numbers of women have the opportunity to attend university and earn advanced theological degrees. Their theologies bring together their experience as women with the theological tradition. In many instances, they follow in the footsteps of our four women Doctors of the Church, refusing to exclude the theology of experience from the theology of the academy. Many forms of liberation theology, done by men as well as women, keep the experience of suffering humanity at the core of their theological work. This theology has as a primary aim to improve the lot of those on the margins. Eschewing the ivory tower, this theology places love of neighbor front and center. In this sense, contemporary theologians have much to learn from the work of the women doctors we have explored.

These Doctors of the Church model a theology that belongs to real life. It is an integrated wisdom theology whose aim is loving action for justice in the world. Thérèse had no patience with truth that did not show itself in deeds. Hildegard viewed the chapel, the garden, the infirmary, the world, the cosmos as related, indeed as the same place, theologically. These women teach us that theology, liturgy and life are all made from the same cloth. They model a sensitivity to evil and a courage to fight for reform in Church and society.

Once the door has been opened to a more existential theology, the audience for theology is significantly broadened. Awareness that the writings of saints such as Catherine, Teresa, and others are truly theological is a great breakthrough. This new consciousness brings with it the possibility that people of faith can view their own spiritual experience through a theological lens. They become empowered to ask theological questions about their experiences and those of the community of faith. What is the Christology, the doctrine of the Trinity, the theology of the Holy Spirit that is embedded in these experiences? These doctors call each of us to lift up out of our experience the latent theology that is present there and then to refine it in a prayerful, intentional way. Who is Christ? What is the meaning of the Trinity? How do I understand sin and grace?

The God Who Loves Madly

Until I began mining the works of women mystics for theological content, I could not have imagined that anyone could write about God's love with the depth and intensity that is visible in these texts. Their language about God is, of course, extremely complex, but in the end, they end up at love. Taken together, the message about God's relentless love grows and gains momentum like a snowball rolling downhill. Their creative attempts to speak of a love that surpasses all understanding caught my attention. It is a commonplace of the Christian tradition that God loves us—even to the cross—but these women expressed this truth in fresh and compelling ways.

For example, both Catherine and Thérèse speak of God as being "madly" in love with humanity, a love that reaches toward folly. Reflecting on the dignity of being made in the image and likeness of God, Catherine wrote: "Why did you so dignify us? With unimaginable love you looked upon your creatures within your very self, and you fell in love with us…. We are your image, and now by making yourself one with us you have become our image, veiling your eternal divinity in the wretched cloud and dung heap of Adam. And why? For Love!"[9] Catherine describes God's as "mad": "You, deep well of charity, it seems you are so madly in love with your creatures that you could not live without us!"[10] In one of her prayers we read:

Oh eternal Trinity!
Eternal Trinity!
Oh Fire and deep well of charity!
Oh you who are madly in love
With your creature![11]

Thérèse, too, prays: "O Jesus, allow me in my boundless gratitude to say to You that Your love reaches unto folly. In the presence of this folly, how can You not desire that my heart leap towards You? How can my confidence, then, have any limits?"[12] Again in Poem 17, she wrote: "Living on Love, what strange folly!" / The world says to me, "Ah! stop your singing. / Don't waste your perfumes, your life. / Learn to use them well…"/…I want to sing on leaving this world: / "I'm dying of love!"[13]

It would be instructive to include a unit on the madness of God's love in our Christian education programs for both adults and children. Do we ever think of God as a "mad lover," and if we did, what response would it elicit from us? These texts bring us back to a motif that is neglected to the point of invisibility. But if we reflect on experiences of intense love, we discover an element of madness that reminds us of the extremes of divine love—the height, depth, length, and width of God's amazing, ineffable, boundless, eternal care for all of creation.

It is not inaccurate to describe these four women as exorbitant in their desire for God and the world. They met a God whose love is excessive and wild and they responded in turn. Their desire was not curtailed by physical and spiritual limitations. Their love for God and the world was focused and uncompromising. Even Thérèse's Little Way was total and intense. Her glimpse of the infinite overflowed into her life—excessive love; lived-out extravagance; transcending boundaries. "She would be doctor and prophet, missionary and martyr; she would be priest and she would go to the ends of the earth, with 'desires…greater than the universe.'"[14]

Christian Anthropology—Reliance on Experience

Throughout this book, we have emphasized the importance of experience and how it influences theology. In sixteenth-century Spain, Teresa of Avila regularly disagrees with advice she is given by spiritual directors when it flies in the face of her experience. She laments having to work with spiritually inexperienced clerical directors who frustrate rather than help her. All the women we have studied insist on the correctness of their positions. No doubt such dispositions are a mix of egoism, stubbornness, or necessity, but beyond these human exigencies, they are a sign of their courage and fidelity to God. We have seen how Hildegard of Bingen approached theology, the Church, music, and medicine in her unique creative way. She is faithful to the Tradition but also has the confidence to expand it, trusting in the vision God had given her. For many holy women, visions provided understanding and insight into theological truths.

These women not only trusted their experience but remained faithful to it at great risk. As noted above, it was radically countercultural for women to take up the pen. It was not as though no one would know or care when they expressed the inherited tradition in a new key, or on occasion raised questions about it. If their texts were intended to circulate only within their religious communities, they found tolerance on the part of Church leadership. But women like Catherine and Teresa who wrote or spoke publicly often had to face a different kind of scrutiny and intolerance, including harrassment and oppression. Teresa of Avila lived under the cloud of the Inquisition.[15] In 1310, in Paris, Marguerite Porete was burned at the stake as a heretic for her book *The Mirror of Simple Souls.* Like Meister Eckhart, her thought pushed against the boundaries of what was considered orthodox. In varying degrees women have been suspect in Church and society.

Embedded in this work is a holistic Christian anthropology that views the entire human person as intrinsically good. In Christ, human beings are virtuous by nature, competent to understand the mysteries of God, and, in spite of sin, called to become one with the divine. These women Doctors also reveal an acute sense of sin and of their nothingness in the face of God's tender, infinite love. But we should not allow this truth to blind us to their confidence in the ability of all Christians to live in grace. Their theological conviction that humans are made in the image and likeness of God leads them to trust in human capabilities for love, virtue, holiness, and theological insight. If it is God's plan and God's will to invite humanity into the very life of the triune God, then it can and will be done. They trusted that because Christ assumed human form, human destiny is to become divine.

Such fidelity to experience can serve as a catalyst to enhance our own. These women challenge us to stand tall, to take ourselves seriously, to appreciate more fully the legacy we share as women doing theology. They invite Christian believers—women and men alike—to attend with reverence to the ways in which God operates in their lives, to trust in these ways, to be emboldened to live them out in spite of obstacles and doubts, and to become "grassroots theologians." The evident assurance of a Hildegard or a Teresa calls us to accountability to our own encounters with life and with God.

These women and their theological work are a source of celebration and pride in the long-buried heritage of strong, holy, intelligent women—models in a time when establishing the full humanity of women is still a major struggle around the globe. Finally, we are grateful for the fresh and, at times, startling insights and images that mark their theologies. Often they are ones we have not heard before. They help us uncover some of the lost truth of our experience and provide a valuable complement to more traditional perspectives.

A Theology Unafraid of Strong Emotion—The Human Christ
The title Doctor of the Church is closely associated with theological teaching and the exercise of intellect. This association is even more pronounced in a society that privileges and rewards the brain over the heart. But those who long for a more holistic understanding of the human person advocate a theology of integration that refuses to diminish the rigors of intellectual work while embracing a central role for the emotions. Theology requires not only thought but also desire, feeling, and love. Our four female Doctors of the Church model a type of theology that incorporates emotion as an integral part of profound theological work.

All possessed the virtue of singleness of purpose—what some call purity of heart. But whether our personalities are Type A or B, we can turn to these women to wake us up emotionally as well as intellectually. Through their own unique journeys, they help us encounter God and develop our theologies through the totality of our existence. More than the theology of the schools, their existential theology explicitly provides intellectual content *embodied* in the emotion of everyday life. This type of theology is dynamic, messy, and creative.

An example of a theology of intense feeling is visible in the fourth mansions of *The Interior Castle* where Teresa says, "The soul experiences deep feelings when it sees itself close to God."[16] Her theology does not ignore, dampen or suppress emotion. Rather, one is overwhelmed by the range and intensity of the affections. The list is extensive—longing, release, joy, delight, contentment, agony, loneliness, tenderness, deprivation, pain, arousal, despair, ecstasy, compassion.

The intensely affective expression of these texts provides a resource for liturgical renewal for planners, participants, and preachers. It embodies the well-worn expression *lex orandi, lex credendi,* i.e., Church teaching is made visible in the celebration of liturgy and prayer. These texts enhance our desire and expectations for prayerful, theologically responsible liturgy.

In particular, they open a door onto the depths of compassion and loving empathy appropriate to the liturgies of Holy Week. Hildegard, Catherine, Teresa, and Thérèse were steeped in the language and music of the liturgy. Hildegard, a composer of liturgical music, wrote: "But I also brought forth songs with their melody, in praise of God and the saints, without being taught by anyone, and I sang them too, even though I had never learnt either musical notation or any kind of singing."[17]

It is tempting and dangerous to allow ourselves to reduce our capacity for feeling to the emoticons on our computers. But the pace of life and methods of communication in our culture pose such a risk. It requires intentional work to reestablish or deepen the affective reservoirs of the faith.

How do we find ways to see and appropriate the feeling behind the intensely affective language used by these women as they face the cross? A first clue is that they related to Jesus as a real, historical human person as well as God. They were truly in love. This cultivated loved relationship led to the kind of aching sorrow and compassion that we experience when anyone we love deeply is suffering. It makes us want to assume the suffering ourselves, even when we know this is not possible. Such emotional knowledge can help us enter into the fullness of Hoy Week rituals. I offer a simple exercise: Take a moment to become silent and centered. Then go to YouTube and listen to a section of Carlo Gesualdo's *Tenebrae Responsories.*[18] In prayerful abandonment to the words and the music, allow yourself to "cross over" and engage the spirit of suffering love found in the texts on the cross by our women Doctors of the Church. An English translation from the Latin is "O all ye that pass by, attend and see if there be any sorrow like unto my sorrow. Attend, O all ye people, and see my sorrow."

The affections are also visible in their compassionate altruism. All four women emphasize as the "bottom line" of their theologies love of neighbor. Regard for the other was the litmus test that marked any genuine theology. At the center of the meaning of incarnation was love of neighbor. These women were servants of the world within and beyond the cloister. They are Christ washing the feet of those around them who are in need. Like Christ, they are prophets, exhibiting enormous courage and risking themselves unto death for a cause to which they passionately dedicated themselves. They invite us to test our theologies through action in the world on behalf of the least among us.

Their embrace of the emotions implicate their bodies as well as their spirits. Their intense engagement with Christ is holistic, encompassing every aspect of their humanity. The passionate, at times erotic, encounters with Christ imbue their Christologies with a distinct flavor that accents Christ's full humanity—his maleness, his feelings of joy and suffering, his body, his vulnerability, and his strength of will.

That these women were not afraid of their emotions should not obscure their intellectual genius. Hildegard towers above others in the breadth and depth of her erudition. Catherine and Thérèse dedicate themselves relentlessly to Truth as the focus of their theological quest. Teresa used the image of a castle to make a stellar contribution to Christology, Christian anthropology, grace, theology of the Trinity, ethics, and theological spirituality.

These women also teach us that theology need not be an irrelevant, bloodless enterprise. They do not ask us to leave either our intellects or our emotions at the door when we enter the world of theological expression. They created theologies that are open not only to the rigors of the mind but also to imagination, verbal play, metaphor, and poetry. Their theologies teach awe and wonder and intense involvement with life. In spite of life-threatening illnesses and internal and external challenges, these Doctors of the Church never lost sight of their ability to be surprised, indeed amazed at the love that God has for them and for all of creation.

Each woman in her unique way left us a theological legacy of prophetic courage. They identified with, and were emboldened by, the Hebrew prophets. They prayed, demanded, pled, and even threatened the Church they loved to be accountable to its mandate to holiness. Teresa and Thérèse were Carmelites, an order steeped in the prophetic tradition of Elijah. Hildegard's visions empowered her to call for reform fuelled by her forceful personality and aristocratic connections. Catherine too had the courage to take what the Spirit asked of her to the public arena.

The Church needed their witness and their voice to confront heresy, to renew virtue, and to offer assurance that God continued to speak to the Church and world. These female prophets experienced the love of God in ways that gave them a rare confidence and certainty, given the limited role afforded women in Church and society. Hildegard received the most explicit and official blessing by the Church. Catherine too, was called upon by popes, cardinals, and nobles who sought her counsel in times of serious crisis.

On the other hand, Teresa of Avila knew firsthand the threat of the Inquisition. She wrote her theology knowing that running afoul of the authorities might mean censure or even death. Thérèse was acutely aware of the failure of priests to live up to their calling and of the threat of atheism. A primary aim of her prayer was for their conversion of heart. The commitment to the truth motivated these women to struggle heroically to understand the depth and nuances of their Spirit-inspired revelations.

In her theological work *Know the Ways of the Lord*, Hildegard railed against the clerical abuse in the Church and laments their lack of virtue. With echoes of Hosea in the background, she hears God speak about unfaithfulness—intended in both literal and metaphorical ways:

> Therefore, O humans, weep and howl to your God, Whom you so often despise in your sinning, when you sow your seed in the worst fornication and thereby become not only fornica- tors but murderers; for you cast aside the mirror of God and

sate your lust at will. Therefore the Devil always incites you to this work, knowing that you desire your lustfulness more than the joy of children.[19]

Hildegard demanded that Church leaders teach true doctrine, which they could not do with their hearts corrupted and closed to justice. She hears God address the offenders as ravenous wolves, holding office by robbery as a wolf cruelly snatches a sheep, doing their own will instead of caring for the sheep. God accuses the offenders whose offense takes on cosmic proportions:

> Therefore, O ye pastors, wail and lament your crimes, which proclaim your iniquity in dire tones, so that the very elements hear their clamor and join in their wailing before My presence. How do you dare to do your office and touch your Lord with bloody hands, in perverse filth and adulterous wickedness? By your uncleanness you shake the foundations of the earth.... Therefore weep and howl, before Death carries you off.[20]

Hildegard's theology of the Church and of the virtues led her to cry out for its conversion.

Catherine of Siena worked to have Pope Gregory XI return to Rome from Avignon where he was under the sway of French royal power. Scandalized by the existence of multiple popes, she wrote in *The Dialogue* the message she heard from God:

> You see well, sweetest daughter, how true it is that they have made a robbers' den of my Church, which is a place of prayer. They sell and buy and have made the grace of the Holy Spirit a piece of merchandise. So you see, those who want the high offices and revenues of the Church buy them by bribing those in charge with money and visions. And those wretches are not concerned about whether [the candidates] are good or bad, but only about pleasing them for love of the gifts they have received. So they make every effort to set these putrid plants in

the garden of holy Church, and for this the wretches will give a good report of them to Christ on earth [i.e., the pope].[21]

Teresa of Avila had to contend with trends in Counter-Reformation Spain that replaced a more open, humanistic piety inspired by Erasmus, and Cardinal Cisneros, with a narrowing atmosphere of suspicion and censorship bolstered by the Inquisition. A growing distrust of personal religious experience threatened the religious authority of women that had developed in the early years of the sixteenth century. In spite of having her writings submitted to the Inquisition at least six times, Teresa had the courage to live a spirituality and create a theology that helped to renew the Church in the post-Reformation era.

While Thérèse of Lisieux lived a much more hidden and enclosed life, she too went on record with prophetic statements admonishing wayward clergy. In addition, she confronted egoism, demolishing our persistent penchant for self-congratulation, spiritual bean-counting, and hubris about being good. Her prophetic voice became more public only after her death, when the community was able to read and analyze her theology. Her consistent choice of the mercy of God over the justice of God—she really subsumes justice into mercy—is part of her prophetic voice that perhaps we have yet to hear clearly. And her illumination of the meaning of suffering in the light of the cross stands as a prophetic beacon to all who would follow in Christ's footsteps to the end.

Their stories, however, are not all courage and conviction. Being open to the gift of prophecy did not shelter these women from occasional, at times severe, self-doubt, discouragement, and even what we would call "depression" today. All were acutely aware of their own sinfulness. Their stories are not ethereal fairy tales, but accounts of real women, many of whom engaged in lifelong struggles within themselves and against forces in Church and society aimed at limiting their spiritual power and means of theological expression. We may sense that the words of encouragement offered to their readers were also intended for themselves, cheering themselves on to stick with the program when the going got rough—as it inevitably did. Such doubt is palpably visible in the texts of Hildegard and Catherine. And yet their drive to reform a lax and corrupt Church enabled them to overcome doubt and fear to speak out against ecclesial abuses in blunt and searing language.

Prophetic theology, as lived by these four women Doctors of the Church, provides insight into a theology of the Holy Spirit. It is the Spirit who provides the ongoing presence of Christ throughout history. These women's experience of Spirit reminds us to attend more explicitly to the role of the Spirit in Christian life and to take note of its rigorous demands. This way is not one of cheap grace. This Spirit theology is grounded in the concrete realities of Church and society, with a marked sensitivity to moral failure and evil forces.

These experiences of Spirit call us back to the biblical truth that the Spirit blows where it chooses (John 3:8)—and that the Spirit calls women as well as men to be Her voice. These women doctors refused to settle for the mediocre, the trivial, or succumb to spiritual apathy (*acedia*). I have admired the courage it took to think and write a word of warning to a sinful world and a Church in disarray. They had to have cared a lot about both to risk so much trying to correct them. They stand as beacons and models of a Spirit-filled power that God offers to all the baptized.

Laity are called by baptism to do theology. Most of us will not write mystical or theological treatises; our letters will not be preserved and bound for future generations of Christians to enjoy. But wherever we find ourselves, we can witness and give voice to our faith. It might be in the family, or at work. It might be while having coffee with a friend, on a retreat, or in a Bible study or prayer group. All of the women we have studied were letter writers, a genre that is at risk in our computer age. Perhaps these holy women will inspire us to take pen to paper (or keystroke to e-mail or text) and "do theology" by sharing insight into the meaning of God's word for our time. There are many ways to witness to the infinite love and care of a God who embraces every atom of creation.

It is also our job to make the theological work of these women more available to the wider Church. Since their reputation for holiness and intellectual acumen already goes far beyond the Roman Catholic Church, and even beyond Christianity, it would be tragic if their own faith community did not know them. Feminism is a primary catalyst for their rediscovery. Women of all faiths, whose religious life has been formed overwhelmingly by male models, are in search of women who provide female guides for life and doctrine.

Naming Catherine, Hildegard, Thérèse, and Teresa as Doctors of the Church is one step toward a more inclusive public theology that incorporates the voices of women. They were creative, competent theologians who fell in love with God, reflected on this experience, and found imagery, metaphors, and concepts to express it in fresh, convincing ways. They also inspire all the baptized to engage in the theological process as "grassroots theologians." We have seen how they responded to the pressing needs and questions of their time and place. We are called to do the same, fully aware that our questions are different, shaped in new ways by subsequent historical developments.

A crucial need in the Church today is open, honest, respectful theological conversation. Such conversations take place at many levels. It happens with friends and family, among professional colleagues, between bishops and thologians, within faith communities, and between the present and the past. These four women Doctors of the Church offer a charismatic theology that involves knowledge of the Scriptures and tradition, creative interpretation, and original, ongoing exploration of ways in which the Christian life and legacy can be put at the service of the world. They combined love, intelligence, reverence, and fidelity to the Bible and Tradition with a concomitant willingness to take risks, to ask hard questions, and to speak the Christian message in new and compelling ways.

Women are more and more a part of this theological calling in the Church. We are grateful for Hildegard, Catherine, Teresa, and Thérèse, who are among the earliest women to tread the path, point the way, endure the potholes, and strew the road with flowers—a gift for our time.

THEOLOGICAL REFLECTION

- How do you as a woman/layperson negotiate the constraints that disempower you as a theologian? What is at stake for you in becoming a "grassroots theologian"? How do you respond to the command: "Do not fear: write"?
- Do you want to share this material with younger women (and men) in the Church? What are some concrete ways to do this?
- Of the four theologies we have studied, to which are you most drawn and why?
- What theological issue most piques your curiosity—Christology? Trinity? Holy Spirit? The human person? Ethics? Creation? Incarnation? Grace? Sin? Other?
- What is the biggest obstacle for you when you read about the theologies of the four women Doctors of the Church?
- What do you see as the most pressing need of the Body of Christ? What prophetic word would you offer?

Hildegard of Bingen

Craine, Renate. *Hildegard: Prophet of the Cosmic Christ.* New York: Crossroad, 1997.

Dreyer, Elizabeth A. *Passionate Spirituality: Hildegard of Bingen and Hadewijch of Brabant.* New York: Paulist, 2005.

———. *Making Sense of God: A Woman's Perspective.* Cincinnati: St. Anthony Messenger Press, 2008.

———. *Holy Power, Holy Presence: Rediscovering Medieval Metaphors for the Holy Spirit.* Mahwah, N.J.: Paulist, 1998.

Hildegard of Bingen. *Scivias.* New York: Paulist, 2007.

———. *Symphonia.* Barbara Newman, trans. Ithaca, N.Y.: Cornell University Press, 1998.

Lachman, Barbara. *The Journal of Hildegard of Bingen: Inspired by a year in the life of the twelfth-century mystic.* New York: Harmony, 1993.

Newman, Barbara. *Sister of Wisdom: St. Hildegard's Theology of the Feminine.* Berkeley, Calif.: University of California Press, 1998.

———, ed. *Voice of the Living Light: Hildegard of Bingen and Her World.* Berkeley, Calif.: University of California Press, 1998.

Sweet, Victoria. *God's Hotel: A Doctor, a Hospital, and a Pilgrimage to the Heart of Medicine.* New York: Riverhead, 2012.

Vision: From the Life of Hildegard von Bingen. Written and directed by Margarethe von Trotta. New York: Zeitgeist Films, 2009.

Winter, Jonah, and Jeanette Winter, illus. *The Secret World of Hildegard.* New York: Arthur A. Levine, 2007. (Children's book).

Catherine of Siena

Brophy, Don. *Catherine of Siena: A Passionate Life.* New York: Blueridge, 2010.

Catherine of Siena. *The Dialogue.* Suzanne Noffke, O.P., trans. Mahwah, N.J.: Paulist, 1980.

Catherine of Siena, *The Letters of St. Catherine of Siena,* Suzanne Noffke, O.P., trans., 4 vols. Tempe, Ariz.: Medieval and Renaissance Texts and Studies, 2000, 2001, 2007, 2008.

———. *The Prayers of Catherine of Siena.* Suzanne Noffke, ed. and trans. New York: Authors Choice, 2001.

Hilkert, Mary Catherine. *Speaking with Authority: Catherine of Siena and the Voices of Women Today.* Mahwah, N.J.: Paulist, 2001.

Luongo, F. Thomas. *The Saintly Politics of Catherine of Siena.* Ithaca, N.Y.: Cornell University Press, 2006.

Noffke, Suzanne. *Catherine of Siena: An Anthology.* 2 vols. Tempe, Ariz.: Arizona Center for Medieval and Renaissance Texts and Studies, 2012.

———. *Catherine of Siena: Vision Through a Distant Eye.* New York: Authors Choice, 1996.

O'Driscoll, Mary, ed., *Passion for the Truth—Compassion for Humanity: Selected Spiritual Writings.* New York: New City, 2005.

Raymond of Capua. *The Life of Catherine of Siena: The Classic on Her Life and Accomplishments as Recorded by Her Spiritual Director.* Charlotte, N.C.: TAN, 2009.

Undset, Sigrid. *Catherine of Siena.* Kate Austin-Lund, trans. San Francisco: Ignatius, 2009.

Teresa of Avila

Ahlgren, Gillian T.W. *Entering Teresa of Avila's Interior Castle: A Reader's Companion.* New York: Paulist, 2005.

_____. *Teresa of Avila and the Politics of Sanctity.* Ithaca, N.Y.: Cornell University Press, 1998.

Bilinkoff, Jodi. *The Avila of Saint Teresa: Religious Reform in a Sixteenth-Century City.* Ithaca, N.Y.: Cornell University Press, 1992.

Dreyer, Elizabeth. *Manifestations of Grace.* Collegeville, Minn.: Liturgical, 1990.

Luti, J. Mary. *Teresa of Avila's Way.* Collegeville, Minn.: Liturgical, 1991.

Medwick, Cathleen. *Teresa of Avila: The Progress of a Soul.* New York: Image, 2001.

Teresa of Avila. *The Interior Castle.* Mahwah, N.J.: Paulist, 1979.

Welch, John. *Spiritual Pilgrims: Carl Jung and Teresa of Avila.* New York: Paulist, 1982.

Williams, Rowan. *Teresa of Avila.* London: Bloomsbury, 2004.

Thérèse of Lisieux

Day, Dorothy. *Thérèse: A Life of Thérèse of Lisieux.* Whitefish, Mont.: Literary Licensing, 2012.

De Meester, Conrad, O.C.D. *With Empty Hands: The Message of St. Thérèse of Lisieux.* Mary Seymour, trans. Washington, D.C.: ICS, 2002.

_____, ed., *Saint Thérèse of Lisieux: Her Life, Times and Teaching.* Washington, D.C.: ICS, 1997.

Payne, Steven. *Saint Thérèse of Lisieux: Doctor of the Universal Church.* Staten Island, N.Y.: St. Paul's, 2002.

Thérèse of Lisieux. *Story of a Soul.* John Clarke, O.C.D., ed. Washington, D.C.: ICS, 1996.

NOTES

Preface

1. Elizabeth A. Dreyer, *Manifestations of Grace* (Collegeville, Minn.: Liturgical, 1990), p.16.
2. Elizabeth A. Johnson, *She Who Is: The Mystery of God in Feminist Theological Discourse* (New York: Crossroad, 1992), p.14.
3. Catherine of Siena, *The Dialogue,* Suzanne Noffke, trans. (Mahwah, N.J.: 1980), p.157.

Chapter One

1. For a list of Doctors of the Church through 1997 see http://www.newadvent.org/cathen/05075a.htm. Hildegard of Bingen and John of Avila were named in 2012.
2. See Bernard McGinn, *The Doctors of the Church: Thirty-Three Men and Women Who Shaped Christianity* (New York: Crossroad, 1999) and Pope Benedict XVI, *Doctors of the Church* (Huntington, Ind.: Our Sunday Visitor, 2011).
3. See Steven Payne, *Saint Thérèse of Lisieux: Doctor of the Universal Church* (Staten Island, New York: St. Paul's, 2002), p. 11. I am indebted to this study for much of the material in this section.
4. See Paul Rorem, "The Company of Medieval Women Theologians," in *Theology Today* 60 (2003): 83. This entire issue is dedicated to medieval Christian women theologians.
5. Ellen T. Charry, "Welcoming Medieval Christian Women Theologians," *Theology Today* 60 (2003): 1.
6. This section contains a number of insights from Rowan Williams's *Why Study the Past: The Quest for the Historical Church* (Grand Rapids: Eerdmans, 2005).
7. See Elizabeth A. Dreyer, *Making Sense of God: A Woman's Perspective* (Cincinnati: Franciscan Media, 2008).
8. Mark McIntosh, *Mysteries of Faith* (Cambridge, Mass.: Cowley, 2000), p. 2.
9. Nicholas Lash, *Theology for Pilgrims* (Notre Dame, Ind.: University of Notre Dame Press, 2008), p. 162.
10. See Barbara Newman, *God and the Goddesses: Vision, Poetry, and Belief in the Middle Ages* (Philadelphia: University of Pennsylvania Press, 2003), pp. 294–304.
11. See Bernard McGinn, *The Flowering of Mysticism: Men and Women in the New Mysticism—1200–1350* (New York: Crossroad, 1998), pp. 19–24.
12. See, for example, the enormous obstacles to women's well-being across the globe chronicled in *Half the Sky: Turning Oppression into Opportunity for Women Worldwide* by Nicholas Kristoff and Cheryl Wu Dunn (New York: Knopf, 2009).

Chapter Two

1. Barbara Newman, ed., *Voice of the Living Light: Hildegard of Bingen and Her World* (Berkeley, Calif.: University of California Press, 1998), p.1. I rely on this volume throughout this chapter.
2. Barbara Newman, "St. Hildegard, Doctor of the Church, and the Fate of Feminist Theology," *Spiritus* 13/1 (Spring 2013): 36, 50.
3. A recent film, *Vision* provides a creative, insightful, contemporary portrayal of Hildegard. This film was written and directed by Margarethe von Trotta, with Barbara Sukowa as Hildegard. Zeitgeist Films, 2009.
4. Between 1177 and 1181, the monks Gottfried of St. Disibod and Dieter of Echternach wrote Hildegard's *Vita,* which contains some personal memoirs dictated by her.
5. See this image in Matthew Fox, *Illuminations of Hildegard of Bingen* (Santa Fe: Bear, 2002), pp. 38, 42.
6. For a compelling account of one example of medical care for the poor in the United States, see Victoria Sweet, *God's Hotel* (New York: Riverhead, 2012). Hildegard figures prominently in this work.
7. See Joy A. Schroeder, "A Fiery Heat: Images of the Holy Spirit in the Writing of Hildegard of Bingen," *Mystics Quarterly* 30/3–4 (2004): 79–98.

8. Hildegard of Bingen, *Scivias*, Mother Columbia Hart and Jane Bishop, trans. (New York: Paulist, 1990), II.4.2.
9. Hildegard, *Scivias*, III.7.9.
10. Hildegard, *Scivias*, II.2.6.
11. Antiphon 26 in Hildegard of Bingen, *Symphonia*, Barbara Newman, trans. (Ithaca, N.Y.: Cornell University Press, 1998), p. 143.
12. Hildegard, *Scivias*, III.11.28
13. For a graphic image of this internal evil, see Fox, *Illuminations*, p. 86.
14. Hildegard, *Scivias*, III.11.13–14. See also Bernard McGinn, *Visions of the End: Apocalyptic Traditions in the Middle Ages*, rev. ed. (New York: Columbia University Press, 1998), p. 101.
15. Hildegard of Bingen, Letter 84r. *The Letters of Hildegard of Bingen* Volume I, Joseph L. Baird and Radd K. Ehrman, trans. (New York: Oxford University Press, 1994), pp. 186–187.
16. The discography for Hildegard is immense. YouTube has a wide range of performances of Hildegard's music. Groups that specialize in accurate reproduction of medieval music include Anonymous 4: *Hildegard von Bingen: 11,000 Virgins: Chants for the Feast of St. Ursula*. Harmonia Mundi. Other texts accompanied by music are performed by Sequentia, *Hildegard von Bingen: Canticle of Ecstasy*. Deutsche Harmonia Mundi.
17. See Newman, *Symphonia*, pp. 141–151.
18. Hildegard of Bingen, *The Book of the Rewards of Life (Liber Vitae Meritorum)*, III, 8. Cited in Barbara Newman, *Sisters of Wisdom: St. Hildegard's Theology of the Feminine* (Berkeley, Calif.: University of California Press, 1987), p. 66.
19. Newman, Antiphon 24, *Symphonia*, p. 141.
20. Newman, Hymn 27, *Symphonia*, pp. 143–147.
21. Newman, Hymn 19, *Symphonia*, pp. 36, 127.
22. *Holistic Healing*, Manfred Pawlik and Patrick Madigan (Collegeville, Minn.: Liturgical, 1994), p. 60.
23. Hildegard, *Vita*, II.6.
24. Hildegard, *Scivias*, I.6.12.
25. Hildegard, *Scivias*, III.4.12.
26. Hildegard, *Scivias*, III.3.7.
27. Hildegard, *Scivias*, II.4.1.
28. Hildegard, *Scivias*, I.1. Prol.
29. Peter Dronke, *Medieval Women Writers of the Middle Ages: A Critical Study of Texts from Perpetua (d. 203) to Marguerite Porete (d. 310)* (Cambridge, U.K.: Cambridge University Press, 1984), p. 201.
30. Sequence 28, *Symphonia*, p. 149.

Chapter Three

1. See Suzanne Noffke, "Catherine of Siena: Justly Doctor of the Church," *Theology Today* 60 (2003): 49–62.
2. For images of Catherine's experience of stigmata see: www.metmuseum.org.
3. For a sampling of artistic renderings of Catherine's mystical marriage go to: www.metmuseum.org.
4. Information on publications at http://www.drawnbylove.com/Suggested%20Reading%20List.htm.
5. To see this image, go to: http://www.casasantapia.com/art/giotto/ognissantimadonna.htm.
6. For a virtual tour of the cathedral, go to: http://www.digital-images.net/Gallery/Scenic/Siena/Cathdrl_Int/cathdrl_int.html.
7. Catherine, *Letters*, IV, 65. Citations are from *The Letters of Catherine of Siena*, Suzanne Noffke, trans., 4 vols. (Tempe, Ariz.: Arizona Center for Medieval and Renaissance Studies, 1988–2008).
8. *Catherine of Siena: The Dialogue*. Suzanne Noffke, trans. (Mahwah, N.J.: Paulist, 1980). References are to paragraph numbers in this text.

9.   Bernard McGinn, *The Varieties of Vernacular Mysticism, 1350-1550* (New York: Crossroad, 2012), pp. 215–216.
10. Catherine, *The Dialogue*, 55.
11. Raymond of Capua, *The Life of Catherine of Siena*, #216, Conleth Kearns, trans. third edition (Collegeville, Minn.: Liturgical, 1980).
12. Catherine, *Letters*, IV, 29–30.
13. Catherine, *Letters*, III, 5.
14. Catherine, *The Dialogue*, 47.
15. Catherine, *The Dialogue*, 55.
16. Catherine, *Letters*, III, 6.
17. Catherine, *Letters*, II, 502.
18. Catherine, *The Dialogue*, 83. See Galatians 3:27.
19. Catherine, Letter to a Florentine abbess, II, pp. 81–82.
20. Catherine, *Letters*, IV, 104.
21. Caroline Walker Bynum, *Fragmentation and Redemption: Essays on Gender and the Human Body in Medieval Religion* (New York: Zone, 1991), p. 222.
22. McGinn, *The Varieties of Vernacular Mysticism*, p. 218. *Apophatic* refers to God's unknowability—God is beyond all language. Its sister concept is *kataphatic*, which refers to using language, imagery, and metaphors to speak of God.
23. McGinn, *The Varieties of Vernacular Mysticism*, p. 208.
24. McGinn, *The Varieties of Vernacular Mysticism*, p. 208.
25. Catherine, *Letters*, IV, 497.
26. Paul VI, *L'Osservatore Romano* (English edition), October 15, 1970, pp. 6–7.
27. Catherine, *Letters*, I, 139, and II, 683.
28. See Suzanne Noffke, *Catherine of Siena: Vision Through a Distant Eye* (Collegeville, Minn.: Liturgical, 1996), p. 27.
29. Catherine, *The Dialogue*, 26–87.
30. Bernard of Clairvaux, *On the Song of Songs I*, 5.1, Kilian Walsh, trans. (Spencer, Mass.: Cistercian, 1971), p. 25.
31. Catherine, *Letters*, II, 498.
32. Catherine, *The Dialogue*, 55.
33. Catherine, *The Dialogue*, 13.
34. Catherine, *The Dialogue*, 147.
35. Catherine, *The Dialogue*, 51.
36. Catherine, *Letters*, III, 312.
37. Catherine, *The Dialogue*, 119; also *The Dialogue*, 23, 134.
38. Catherine, *The Dialogue*, 43.
39. Suzanne Noffke, *The Prayers of Catherine of Siena*, second ed., (San Jose: Authors Choice Press, 2001), Prayer 10, p. 84.
40. Suzanne Noffke, *Catherine of Siena*, p. 18.
41. Catherine, *The Dialogue*, 72.
42. Catherine, *Letters*, II, 2.
43. Catherine, *The Dialogue*, 27.
44. Catherine, *The Dialogue*, 55.
45. Catherine, *The Dialogue*, 25–26.
46. For Catherine's theology of the Trinity, see Elizabeth A. Dreyer, *Holy Power, Holy Presence: Rediscovering Medieval Metaphors for the Holy Spirit* (Mahwah, N.J.: Paulist, 2007), pp. 186–190.
47. Catherine, *The Dialogue*, 110.
48. One example is Catherine Mowry LaCugna, *God For Us: The Trinity & Christian Life* (San Francisco: HarperSanFrancisco, 1991).
49. Search Google Images for "Picasso, La Ronde de la Jeunesse" to view the image.
50. Catherine, *The Dialogue*, 7.
51. Catherine, *The Dialogue*, 85.
52. Catherine, *Letters*, III, 307.
53. Catherine, *Letters*, IV, 438.

54. Caroline Walker Bynum, *Fragmentation and Redemption*, p. 172.
55. Catherine, *Letters,* II, 502.
56. Catherine, *Letters,* II, 495.
57. Catherine, *Letters,* IV, 139.
58. Catherine, *Letters,* II, 504.
59. Noffke, *Catherine of Siena*, p. 63.
60. Catherine, *Letters,* II, 499.
61. Catherine, *Letters,* I, 10, 92, p. 85.

Chapter Four
1. Search Google Images for "Teresa of Avila" for a range of images.
2. Cited in *Teresa of Avila and the Rhetoric of Femininity* by Alison Weber (Princeton, N.J.: Princeton University Press, 1990), pp. 3–4. Biblical passages enjoining silence on women include: 1 Corinthians 14:34; 1 Timothy 2:11; 2 Timothy 3:6–7.
3. For a lecture at Notre Dame on Teresa of Avila as Doctor of the Church, see Keith Egan at http://www.youtube.com/watch?v=gd77qwAwkfc. See also Keith Egan, "The Significance for Theology of the Doctor of the Church: Teresa of Avila," in *The Pedagogy of God's Image: Essays on Symbol and the Religious Imagination*, Robert Masson, ed. The Annual Publication of the College Theology Society (Chico, Calif.: Scholars, 1981), pp. 153–171.
4. For a video of Avila and its buildings related to Teresa and a selection of well-known images of her, see: http://www.youtube.com/watch?v=zEW6l4CBD3o.
5. Teresa of Avila, *Interior Castle*, VI.4.10.
6. Reformed Carmelites were known as "discalced" because they wore sandals without stockings. The original group became known as the "calced" or "shod."
7. Alison Weber, *Teresa of Avila and the Rhetoric of Femininity* (Princeton, N.J.: Princeton University Press, 1990), p. 163.
8. J. Mary Luti, *Teresa of Avila's Way* (Collegeville, Minn.: Liturgical, 1991), p. 58.
9. Converted Muslims were called *moriscos;* converted Jews were called *conversos.*
10. Teresa of Avila, *Interior Castle*, III.1.2.
11. Teresa of Avila, *Interior Castle*, VI.7.6.
12. Rowan Williams, *Teresa of Avila* (London: Continuum, 1991), p. 37.
13. Teresa of Avila, *Interior Castle*, III.1.5.
14. Teresa of Avila, *The Book of Her Life*, 19.4, in *The Collected Works of St. Teresa of Avila*, Vol. 1, Kieran Kavanaugh and Otilio Rodriguez, trans. (Washington, D.C.: ICS, 1976).
15. Teresa of Avila, *Interior Castle*, I.1.2.
16. Rowan Williams, *Teresa of Avila*, pp. 115–116.
17. Teresa of Avila, *The Way of Perfection* 28.11, in *The Collected Works of St. Teresa of Avila*, Vol. 2, Otilio Rodriguez and Kieran Kavanaugh, trans. (Washington, D.C.: ICS, 1980).
18. Teresa of Avila, *Interior Castle*, I.1.1.
19. Teresa of Avila, *The Way of Perfection,* 28.11.
20. Teresa of Avila, *The Way of Perfection,* 28.12.
21. Teresa of Avila, *Interior Castle*, III.1.5–6.
22. Teresa of Avila, *Interior Castle*, III.1.7.
23. Teresa of Avila, *The Book of Her Life,* 10.6.
24. Teresa of Avila, *Interior Castle*, I.1.2.
25. Rowan Williams, *Teresa of Avila*, pp. 52–53.
26. Teresa of Avila, *The Book of Her Life,* 11.4.
27. See John 14.2; *Interior Castle*, I.1.8.
28. Teresa of Avila, *Foundations*, 5.2, in *The Collected Works of St. Teresa of Avila*, Vol. 3, Otilio Rodriguez and Kieran Kavanaugh, trans. (Washington, D.C.: ICS, 1985).
29. Teresa of Avila, *The Book of Her Life,* 13.13.
30. Teresa of Avila, *Interior Castle*, VII.1.6.
31. Teresa of Avila, *Interior Castle*, 5.3.11–12.
32. Teresa of Avila, *The Book of Her Life,* 11.6.
33. Teresa of Avila, *The Book of Her Life,* 11.7.
34. Teresa of Avila, *The Book of Her Life,* 14.2.

35. Teresa of Avila, *The Book of Her Life*, 14.10.
36. Teresa of Avila, *The Book of Her Life*, 16.1.
37. Teresa of Avila, *The Book of Her Life*, 16.3.
38. Teresa of Avila, *The Book of Her Life*, 19.1.
39. See Gian Lorenzo Bernini's famous sculpture of Teresa in ecstasy: http://en.wikipedia.org/wiki/Ecstasy_of_Saint_Teresa.
40. Teresa of Avila, *The Book of Her Life*, 18. 3.
41. Teresa of Avila, *Interior Castle*, II.1.3.
42. Teresa of Avila, *The Book of Her Life*, 18.14.
43. Teresa of Avila, *The Book of Her Life*, 19.3.
44. Teresa of Avila, *Interior Castle*, VI.7.8.
45. Teresa of Avila, *Testimonies* in *The Collected Works of St. Teresa of Avila*, Vol. 1, Kieran Kavanaugh and Otilio Rodriguez, trans. (Washington, D.C.: ICS, 1976), p. 24.
46. Teresa of Avila, *Interior Castle*, V.2.5–6.
47. *Testimonies*, 49.
48. Teresa of Avila, *Interior Castle*, V.1.7.
49. Teresa of Avila, *The Book of Her Life*, 10.6.
50. Teresa of Avila, *Interior Castle*, I.2.3.
51. Teresa of Avila, *Interior Castle*, I.2.9.
52. Teresa of Avila, *Interior Castle*, I.2.10.
53. Teresa of Avila, *The Book of Her Life*, 7.17.
54. Teresa of Avila, *The Book of Her Life*, 7.11.
55. Teresa of Avila, *Interior Castle*, I.1.3.
56. Teresa of Avila, *The Book of Her Life*, 4.2
57. Teresa of Avila, *The Book of Her Life*, 8.7.
58. Teresa of Avila, *The Book of Her Life*, 7.19.
59. Teresa of Avila, *Interior Castle*, I.2.17.
60. Teresa of Avila, *Interior Castle*, VI.5.3.
61. Teresa of Avila, *The Book of Her Life*, 18.4; 19.4; *Interior Castle*, V.3.1.
62. Teresa of Avila, *Meditations on the Song of Songs*, 7.3, in *The Collected Works of St. Teresa of Avila*, Vol. 2, Otilio Rodriguez and Kieran Kavanaugh, trans. (Washington, D.C.: ICS, 1980).
63. Teresa of Avila, *Interior Castle*, V.3.8.
64. Teresa of Avila, *Interior Castle*, II.1.6 and 10.
65. Teresa of Avila, *The Book of Her Life*, 7.20.
66. Teresa of Avila, *The Book of Her Life*, 34.16.
67. Teresa of Avila, *The Book of Her Life*, 8:5.
68. Skobhán Garrigan, "Teresa of Ávila (1515–82)" in *The Blackwell Companion to the Theologians*, Vol. 1, Ian S. Markham, ed. (Malden, Mass.: Wiley-Blackwell, 2009), p. 388.
69. Teresa of Avila, *Interior Castle*, V.4.11.
70. Cited in Weber, *Teresa of Avila and the Rhetoric of Femininity*, pp. 164–165.
71. Teresa of Avila, *The Way of Perfection*, 22.3–4.
72. Teresa of Avila, *The Way of Perfection*, 21.1.
73. Teresa of Avila, *The Book of Her Life*, 10.4.
74. Teresa of Avila, *Interior Castle*, I.1.4.
75. T.S. Eliot, *Four Quartets*, "East Coker," V.
76. Teresa of Avila, *The Way of Perfection*, 21.2.
77. Teresa of Avila, *The Way of Perfection*, 21.2.
78. Teresa of Avila, *The Book of Her Life*, 40.3.
79. Gillian T.W. Ahlgren, *Entering Teresa of Avila's Castle: A Reader's Companion* (New York: Paulist, 2005), p. 122.
80. Karl Rahner, "Teresa of Avila: Doctor of the Church," in Karl Rahner, *Opportunities for Faith: Elements of a Modern Spirituality*, Edward Quinn, trans. (New York: Seabury, 1970), p. 126.
81. Teresa of Avila, *Interior Castle*, VII.1.1.

82. Teresa of Avila, *Interior Castle*, VII.2.1 and VII.3.2.

83. *Interior Castle*, Epilogue.

Chapter Five

1. Joseph F. Schmidt, *Everything Is Grace: The Life and Way of Thérèse of Lisieux* (Frederick, Md.: Word Among Us, 2007), p. 12.

2. For a critical perspective on Thérèse's doctorate see William C. Graham, "Is There a Case Against Saint Thérèse as Doctor of the Church?" *Sisters Today* 67 (January 1995): 57.

3. Search Google Images for "Thérèse of Lisieux" for a range of images. Also go to YouTube and search "Thérèse of Lisieux and James Martin, S.J."

4. *The Story of a Soul: The Autobiography of Thérèse of Lisieux*. John Clarke, trans. (Washington D.C.: ICS, 2002), is made up of three distinct parts: (1) Chapters 1–8 recount the story of her life requested by Mother Agnes early in 1895 (Manuscript A); (2) Chapter 9 is a letter to her sister Marie written in 1896 (Manuscript B); (3) Chapters 10–11 complete her life story, requested by Mother Marie de Gonzague in 1897 (Manuscript C).

5. Read Thérèse's entire corpus at http://archives-carmel-lisieux.fr/english/carmel/index. php?option=com_content&view=article&id=2124&Itemid=101.

6. Since Thérèse's sister Pauline also edited Thérèse's works after Thérèse died, scholars have been hard at work on the original autographs to identify editorial changes that altered or obscured Thérèse's own ideas. Over the course of time, we have come closer to the genuine thought of Thérèse.

7. This event is the subject of Gertrud von Le Fort's novella, *Song at the Scaffold* (1931); Rev. R. Bruckberger produced a film with dialogue by Georges Bernanos (1937); later Bernanos composed a libretto, *Dialogues of the Carmelites* (1949); an opera of the same title was composed by Francis Poulenc, based on this libretto (1957).

8. For images of this period see: http://www.indiana.edu/~b357/slides%202012/ lecture%2014%20(Franco-Prussian%20war%20commune).pdf.

9. Thomas Nevin, *Thérèse of Lisieux: God's Gentle Warrior* (Oxford, U.K.: Oxford University Press, 2006), p. 56.

10. Dom Guéranger, *The Liturgical Year*, fifteen volumes, nine of which were written by the author between 1841 and 1875. The remaining volumes were written by another Benedictine under Guéranger's name (London: St. Austin, 2000).

11. Ida Görres, *The Hidden Face: A Study of St. Thérèse of Lisieux* (London: Burns and Oates, 1959), p. 139.

12. Thérèse of Lisieux, *Story of a Soul*, p. 179.

13. John Paul II, "Divini Amoris Scientia: Apostolic Letter," no. 8, *Origins* 27 (20 November 1997): 390–396.

14. For a two-minute video of this lovely home, go to http://www.youtube.com/watch? v=numEafuenas.

15. Thérèse was drawn to, and formed by, the ideas in Thomas à Kempis's *Imitation of Christ*, which was popular at the time. This book provided beleaguered Roman Catholics with a way to deal with the indifference and hostility of nineteenth-century France toward the Church. The *Imitation* emphasizes the inevitability of suffering and the need to embrace it as part of the spiritual journey. Thérèse's ideas about heaven were influenced by a book given to her father, M. Martin, titled *The End of this World and Mysteries of the Life to Come*. Thérèse read this book in 1887 and described it as "one of my life's greatest blessings." It spoke of the heavenly rewards that would be in store for those who chose a life of sacrifice.

16. Three other sisters in the house also had "the Holy Face" in their religious names: Sr. C. Geneviève, Sr. L.J. Marie and Sr. Marie F. Th. of the Child Jesus.

17. See *General Correspondence*, Vol. I, 1877–1890, John Clarke, trans. (Washington, D.C.: Institute of Carmelite Studies, 1982 and 1988), Letter 91.

18. Thérèse of Lisieux, *Story of a Soul*, p. 41.

19. See Mary Frohlich, "A Spirituality for Times of Illness: The Case of Thérèse of Lisieux," *New Theology Review* 14/4 (November 2001): 32–43.

20. Thérèse of Lisieux, *Story of a Soul,* pp. 58–60.

21. Thérèse of Lisieux, *Story of a Soul,* p. 149.

22. See Claude Langlois, *Le désir de sacerdoce chez Thérèse de Lisieux suivi par les trois vies de Thérèse au Carmel* (Paris: Editions Salvator, 2002).

23. Ida Görres, *The Hidden Face: A Study of St. Thérèse of Lisieux* (London: Burns and Oates, 1959), p. 139.

24. At the age of twelve, Thérèse and her family became members of The Atoning Confraternity of the Holy Face. For a psychological perspective on the Holy Face, see Mary Frohlich, *Your Face Is My Only Homeland: A Psychological Perspective on Thérèse of Lisieux and Devotion to the Holy Face,* ed. David M. Hammond (New London, Conn.: Twenty-Third, 2000), pp. 177–205.

25. Surprisingly, the idea of the "Little Way" is first mentioned in 1894 and Thérèse used this exact phrase only once.

26. Thérèse of Lisieux, Prayer 12. *The Prayers of Thérèse of Lisieux: Critical Edition of the Complete Works of Saint Thérèse of the Child Jesus and of the Holy Face.* Aletheia Kane, trans. (Washington, D.C.: ICS, 1997), p. 91.

27. This verse (Song 5:2) was written on the wall of the St. Elias cell wing of Carmel.

28. See Geneviève of the Holy Face, *A Memoir of My Sister St. Thérèse* (New York: P.J. Kenedy & Sons, 1959), pp. 111–112, cited in Steven Payne, *Saint Thérèse of Lisieux; Doctor of the Universal Church* (New York: Alba House, 2002), pp. 44–45. It would be interesting to know what Thérèse would have thought about the fact that between 1898 and 1925, 328,000 pictures of her had been distributed. See Guy Gaucher, *The Story of a Life* (San Francisco: HarperSanFrancisco, 1987), p. 211, cited in Payne, p. 63, n. 61.

29. Steven Payne, p. 68, n. 75. The story of the pictures of Thérèse's "face" is complex. As Céline aged, her new portraits of Thérèse became more and more idealized and are considered by most critics today as overly sentimental. When an annotated edition of the un-retouched photos was published in 1961, some accused Céline of falsifying Thérèse's true face. A more benign assessment acknowledges that Céline was simply following the tastes of her time and context. See *The Photo Album of St. Thérèse of Lisieux,* commentary by François de Sainte-Marie, Peter-Thomas Rohrback, trans. (New York: P.J. Kenedy & Sons, 1962).

30. Cited in Görres, *The Hidden Face,* p. 206.

31. Hans Urs von Balthasar, *Thérèse of Lisieux: The Story of a Mission* (London: Sheed and Ward, 1953), p. 157.

32. André Combes, *St. Thérèse and Her Mission: The Basic Principles of Theresian Spirituality,* Alastair Guinan, trans. (New York: P.J. Kenedy & Sons, 1955), p. 88.

33. *General Correspondence,* Letter 63, p. 460.

34. Thérèse of Lisieux, Letter 96, Vol. 1, p. 587.

35. Thomas Nevin, *Thérèse of Lisieux,* p. 56.

36. For an insightful analysis of the theme of facing, including a chapter on Thérèse of Lisieux, see David F. Ford, *Self and Salvation: Being Transformed,* Cambridge Studies in Christian Doctrine (Cambridge: Cambridge University Press, 1999), pp. 167–240.

37. Thérèse of Lisieux, *Story of a Soul,* p. 192.

38. Thérèse of Lisieux, *Story of a Soul,* p. 193.

39. Letter 224. See also poems "Canticle to Obtain the Canonization of Joan of Arc," and "To Joan of Arc" in *The Poetry of Saint Thérèse of Lisieux,* Donald Kinney, trans. (Washington, D.C.: ICS, 1996), pp. 46, 199.

40. *St. Thérèse of Lisieux: Her Last Conversations,* May 27, 1897, John Clarke, trans. (Washington, D.C.: ICS, 1977), p. 51.

41. Thérèse of Lisieux, Poem 32.

42. Thérèse of Lisieux, Prayer 14.

43. Thérèse of Lisieux, Poem 36.

44. Thérèse of Lisieux, Letter 96.

45. See especially Thérèse of Lisieux, Letters 83, 94, 96, 108, 120, 137, 142, and 169.

46. Thérèse of Lisieux, Letter 82.

47. Thérèse of Lisieux, Letter 89.

48. *St. Thérèse of Lisieux: Her Last Conversations*, p. 52.
49. Thérèse of Lisieux, Poem 20.
50. Simon Tugwell, "St. Thérèse of Lisieux," *Doctrine and Life*, 33 (1983): 340.
51. Thérèse of Lisieux, Prayer 6.
52. *St. Thérèse of Lisieux: Her Last Conversations*, p. 183.
53. Thérèse of Lisieux, Poem 45.
54. Thérèse of Lisieux, Prayer 17.
55. For a treatment of six medieval theologies of the cross, see Elizabeth A. Dreyer, ed., *The Cross in Christian Tradition: Paul to Bonaventure* (Mahwah, N.J.: Paulist, 2000).
56. Thérèse invokes the name of Jesus sixteen hundred times in her writings.
57. Thérèse of Lisieux, *Story of a Soul*, pp. 196–197.
58. Thérèse's radical abandonment of self-will is reminiscent of the thirteenth-century Beguines, Mechthild of Magdeburg, Hadewijch of Brabant and Marguerite Porete and the Dominican Meister Eckhart. Each advocated a total annihilation of self in order to become one with God.
59. Mary Frohlich, "Desolation and Doctrine in Thérèse of Lisieux," *Theological Studies* 61 (2000): 264.
60. Recent secular analyses of the blessings of failure include Kathryn Schultz, *Being Wrong: Adventures in the Margin of Error* (New York: Ecco, 2010); and Dr. Norman E. Rosenthal, *The Gift of Adversity: The Unexpected Benefits of Life's Difficulties, Setbacks and Imperfections* (New York: Tarcher, 2013).
61. Thérèse of Lisieux, Poem 17.

Chapter Six
1. Emily A. Holmes and Wendy Farley, eds., *Women, Writing, Theology: Transforming a Tradition of Exclusion* (Waco, Tex.: Baylor University Press, 2011), p. 3. I am indebted to this introduction for material in this paragraph.
2. Wendy Farley, "Postscript: Wounded Writing, Healing Writing," in *Women, Writing, Theology*, p. 253.
3. Wendy Farley, *The Wounding and Healing of Desire: Weaving Heaven and Earth* (Louisville, Ky.: Westminster John Knox, 2005), p. xiii.
4. I refer in this section to suffering that is experienced in the course of an ordinary life that ranges from minor to severe. What follows does not apply to catastrophic suffering, such as prolonged torture that has as its sole aim the total destruction of the human person. See Elaine Scarry, *The Body in Pain: The Making and Unmaking of the World* (Oxford, U.K.: Oxford University Press, 1987).
5. Constance Fitzgerald, "The Mission of Thérèse of Lisieux," *The Way Supplement* 89 (1997), 96, n. 33.
6. Catherine, *The Dialogue*, 47.
7. Catherine, *The Dialogue*, 14, see also 15.
8. See Catherine, *The Dialogue*, 75, and Letter T16. I thank Suzanne Noffke for calling my attention to this insight.
9. Catherine, *The Dialogue*, 13.
10. Catherine, *The Dialogue*, 25.
11. Prayer 10, from Catherine of Siena, *The Prayers of Catherine of Siena*, 2nd edition, translated and edited by Suzanne Noffke (San Jose: Authors Choice, 2001), p. 83.
12. Thérèse of Lisieux, *Story of a Soul*, p. 200.
13. Thérèse of Lisieux, *The Poetry of Saint Thérèse of Lisieux*, Donald Kinney, trans. (Washington, D.C.: ICS, 1995), p. 87.
14. Constance Fitzgerald, "The Mission of Thérèse of Lisieux," p. 91. The citation is from *Story of a Soul*, p. 192.
15. See Alison Weber, *Teresa of Avila and the Rhetoric of Femininity* (Princeton, N.J.: Princeton University Press, 1990).
16. Teresa of Avila, *Interior Castle*, IV.3.12.
17. Hildegard of Bingen, *Vita*. Cited in Peter Dronke, *Medieval Women Writers* (Cambridge, U.K.: Cambridge University Press, 1984), p. 145.

18. Carlo Gesualdo (1566–1613), an Italian Renaissance composer, wrote secular madrigals and the deeply moving lamentations, *Tenebrae Responsories,* heard at http://www.youtube.com/watch?v=ntrb_86cUok.
19. See Hildegard, *Scivias,* 84.
20. Hildegard, *Scivias,* 286.
21. Catherine, *The Dialogue,* 249.

ABOUT THE AUTHOR

ELIZABETH A. DREYER is professor emerita of religious studies at Fairfield University in Connecticut, and an adjunct professor at the Hartford Seminary. She is the author or editor of nine books, including *Making Sense of God: A Woman's Perspective,* and has written extensively on topics such as medieval theology and spirituality, women's spirituality, and contemporary lay spirituality.